T0123342

Brown Beauty

Random Thoughts of a 7th Grader

Tamana Izat

authorHOUSE®

AuthorHouse™
1663 Liberty Drive
Bloomington, IN 47403
www.authorhouse.com
Phone: 1 (800) 839-8640

No part of this book may be reproduced, stored in a retrieval system, or transmitted by any means without the written permission of the author.

Published by AuthorHouse 08/17/2018

ISBN: 978-1-5462-5578-9 (sc)
ISBN: 978-1-5462-5579-6 (e)

Print information available on the last page.

Any people depicted in stock imagery provided by Getty Images are models, and such images are being used for illustrative purposes only. Certain stock imagery © Getty Images.

This book is printed on acid-free paper.

Because of the dynamic nature of the Internet, any web addresses or links contained in this book may have changed since publication and may no longer be valid. The views expressed in this work are solely those of the author and do not necessarily reflect the views of the publisher, and the publisher hereby disclaims any responsibility for them.

My father was white, my mother was white, my sisters were white and I was brown. I failed to understand this differentiation, and this Analogy of discretion based on color. Why? I don't know. I didn't know then but I know now. I was born to a couple of brown father married to a white mother. Both wanted me to be happy. Outrageous. Is it not? How can I be happy or how can anybody be happy in a situation like this and do you know, to be happy is a relative term, i.e. happier than less-happier, more-happier than simply happier. I may be happy for the same reasons against which, others could be unhappy. I was born to an Abusive father. what a family to land in.

I was born and raised in a great country. In some remote village recorded on my birth certificate. I don't know where it is or where it was. I could not even care to locate it. In the city map. No, it was not a city or town and definitely some village in the suburb. When I will recollect the name, who would know. I don't know for sure, I will then google search it later, in leisure times. My birth was unexpected I was told. Unexpected? Why unexpected?

Births are always expected. Births are always presumed to happen. A happening which you expect, cannot be unexpected. It can't be assumed or guessed or better still forecasted. Anyhow I came to this world unexpectedly. I was a product of a broken home. Naturally leading to a broken childhood. Not necessarily to live on streets but without a permanent residence. I was shifting residencies. Not within a locality, city or country. I was shifting residences in between continents. From America to Asia, back to America, back to Asia and it went on.

I was told shift of residence and change of school are considered, identified, declared as crisis events for a child. I didn't face any crisis. It is not a crisis to be documented or even mentioned in casual talk. There was no crisis. It was a routine to me. A routine without which I could have felt out of place. My mother litigated her citizenship status out of the provisions of VAWA, a secondary amendment to our constitution. That time I was not even aware of constitution, leave alone the first, the second, the third or any number of amendments added or subtracted from the original constitution of the nation.

A nation prospered out of diversity. Diversity of cultures, traditions and civilizations. How can so many casts, creeds, faiths and colors can exist or coexist in a country at any given time. A country which had the pride to claim itself to be great. Great, fulfilling great but empty within, poor deep down and wealthy, filthy rich country full of homeless people growing in number like the prosperity of this country.

Good thing I was not diagnosed a case of Attention Deficit Hyperactivity disorder but I believe, rather I was told, I was a restless child. I refused mother's milk and turned out a cry-some baby. I will cry and cry to get hungry still refusing milk, mother's or bottle's, I didn't know how I could have lived, survived and grown if not to have been diagnosed a case of lactose intolerance. Good thing not intolerance to stupidity. I was a stupid child to have refused milk. I don't think this was a story, I could have remembered as a kid. Must have been told to me my elders. Who are elders? I don't know. I'm not sure. My Grandmother once casually told me that I have been exchanged in the hospital after birth. Some stupid nurse must have mistakenly put the hospital foot-band label on me belonging to somebody else.

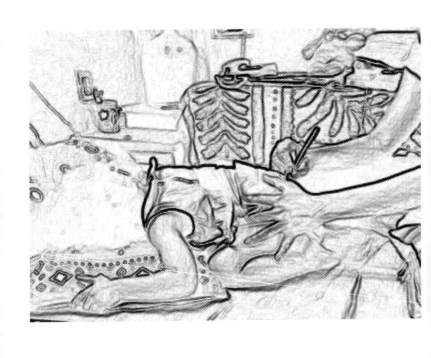

These were casual remarks told in some cultures to teach children. I was not believing it. In spite of believing it. Momma casually signed on my diaper when I was asleep with my bottom up to probably rest assure me that I was her child. Why to worry now? I would know in the end. And now the fact that I am a seventh-grade student, studying in a state sponsored public school being tutored at Home to cope up with the lack of luxury of private schools in absentia and nobody to help me to cope-up with the ever-increasing homework load of studies, which I was supposed to digest, in-spite of paucity of time allocated for my homework.

I was also obliged to share the petty menial house hold chores as a routine more-so becoming a compulsion after the birth of my younger sister, 8 to 9 years younger to me. I had another white elder sister older tome by 8 to 9 years, who lived elsewhere. I fail to understand the gap of so many years among sisters more so one white and one brown. I was almost living with the feelings of insecurity. Insecurity leading to emotional turmoil, as some elders say. But who are my elders. My white father? Who goes from place to place, from dawn to dusk and to return to work from home all night.

My white mother who no doubt is my genuine well-wisher but has no time for me. As she had to get up early, make breakfast for the unit, serve breakfast to the unit, pack lunches for the unit, help the unit to keep the essentials before sending off and to rush to attend to her business routine of ethnic costumes for south Asian community, running an elegant boutique in a busy city center also to follow the school visits, visits to accountants, visits for groceries, visits to her parent-in-laws, visits to immigrant parents, all very tiring and taxing with additional nagging and complaining attitude of her parents taking all her time.

My white sister asking her for her time, my white father asking for her turn. Her foolish assistant asking for her time and the so called esteemed clients asking for her time. I can understand she will not find time for me. She won't be left for no time for anyone. I have learned to live without her time and attention, distracted all along. My elders? Again, who are they? They can't be one of my paternal grandfather who leaves Home while I'm sleeping and returns home while I'm sleeping.

They can't be one of my paternal Grandmother who has all the time in the world. But for her commitments to friends and other activities. She believes she has created fame for herself. My elder can't be my surrogate mother and aunt who is brown and her husband who is brown, who are biased, immersed in their computers do not have time to take a breath even, to leave alone me. My elders can't be one of my brown Uncle and his brown wife who live seven seas apart and busy in their own preoccupation. My elders can't be my brown grand-mother of maternal side who sleeps late, get up late, get late in cooking and house hold duties, get late for her school, get late for watching TV serials.

Naturally I am left with one brown person who had been my watch dog, to reverse the spelling, watch god, sorry I mean Watch Guard and my guardian since long to whom I have nick named 'Guard' for the convenience of writing, spelling, speaking, whispering, confiding and clinging. He was a frustrated celebrity of his time. Had had a profession, a faculty of his own and now became an author and writing books after books getting lost in editing and may continue till he dies. May even continue after his death as much as he wishes.

So, I'm left with nothing from brown to white color all admixture of interesting shades. Some were dark brownish, some light brown, some grayish white and some whitish grey. Brownish were brownish, sheepish and squeamish. Whites were supremist, fascists, and racists. Let them be. I can't help. I don't want to help. I know with passage of time Browns will become racists some time in future. That is how history works, of course not geography, but how does it matter. As of now.

Only now I can understand why Martin Luther king or Malcom X or Mandela or others must have raised their voices, protest and given sacrifices in their life-times. My white elders were eager to show off my white sister almost letting me to live with a feeling of having been neglected. They did open partiality and I felt dejected. They laid open arms for her and I felt jealous. My Grandmother was talking about sibling rivalry as if I am on the opposite side of the fence or concrete borders ready to wage wars against each other. They were wrong. They are misunderstood.

They didn't understand children. They must have grown up from toddlers to adults without any childhood. They don't know children. Children are a different kind of species as though amphibians, Pisces, Aries or some unknown creatures of God. In actual fact they can't understand they are different. A different kind of special caste and creed in themselves and I don't want to understand them.

All were abusers and buffoons in my books and they all need help of counselors. They all must be submitted to group therapy of deviant elders by selective counseling. Another abused person, my Guard was understanding, he knew my anger, he dealt with my anger and managed with my anger. I used to ask him difficult questions and I found him ready with some justifiable answers. He was good in concocting answers. They were always available with him as ready-made decoction to be swallowed and to get nullified.

I would ask about the proof of the existence of God, and he would reply by the signs which I see around. I would ask what language Adam and Eve would have conversed. Was it sign language or some gibberish which only they can understand and converse. Why when there were no other people existed in those early times and families to exchange proposals of the children in the community, how the mankind multiplied. Why grown up individuals used to worship idols which they themselves have made. Why God created this world, and how come one world got divided into many countries. What was the purpose of creation of mankind, what is expected out of them, why did God intend to create so many sects, castes and creeds. What is mankind doing to serve the purpose of life and am there must be some very sensible reason for it.

I was always full of questions and poor Guard was not always ready with answers. Mostly he was lacking in answers and he would either bite betel nuts or light his pipe, to gain time. He would get more time when he is chewing on betel nuts, as he would point his finger to his mouth indicating he cannot speak until the process is over. He was a character. I was notified that later I would have to learn gender education. I was not able to understand the reason or the purpose behind this expected challenge. Any thing which we are not acquainted would remain a challenge.

I knew there are two genders, both for different roles and responsibilities. But for what? What is the big deal in it? No big deal. I knew girls and boys. Both are alike except that girls have longer hair and boys are short cutters. Both of us are a grade higher than animals and we have to behave accordingly. Not like herds of cattle. We have to have assembly in the morning, followed by classes in different subjects and followed by discipline training and games and fun and frolics. But that does not need any special course or exam for that matter.

There were good boys and bad boys, good girls and bad girls, likewise there are teachers good and bad, gatekeepers good and bad, orderlies good and bad. I asked Guard this question.

'What do you mean', was his question back to me.

'I mean what is gender education going to be and for what'?

'Education is for learning the differences in structures and their function'. It was a curt reply.

I thought he didn't want to pursue this subject. I changed it. I asked him.

'Guard, I have heard of love and greed many times, what is it'?

He lighted his pipe. I knew I have to wait.

'See lady, love is like dove of wheat powder to bake into bread or cake and greed is coating, coloring, icing and decoration'.

'That means greed is better, is it not.'

'No not really or maybe, I don't know' he said and swallowed betel nuts. He had a way of escaping from probing or difficult questions. He could easily escape replying on some pretext or the other. Especially the leading questions. He sometime becomes Guarded in replying to my questions. Guard being Guarded, what an irony in itself. How does it matter?

I was born in US and the trend of the place is to get acquainted with words like bitches, red necks, black skins and yellow race. To native American they call red Indians still.

This place is full of racists. All were retarded and morons.

'Kids are not supposed to speak like this' my Momma cried. She wanted to be a good mother of good children. She loved me in her guarded way. She may not have been loved by her parents, the way she expected. Guarded mother was the daughter of Guard.

Everyone seemed guarded. Pleasant but guarded. She was a pretty person and I was not so pretty. I knew the difference. Her behavior was ladylike and my attitude was that of a rowdy sheeter. She has Victorian mannerisms and I had Dravidian mannerisms. She was best suited to be crowned 'Miss. World' and I was good to be just an orderly. She was active and I was lazy, she was smart and I was dull, she was intelligent and I was backward and she was the abused and I was the abuser.

My Dad was an impartial person. He gave no more attention to my younger sister than to me, in his own guarded way. I used to argue with him for my wants and poor fellow, he would accept defeat easily. I was always trying to dominate and he was usually yielding to me. He would be busy working on computer and I would be watching video games on iPad. He had two iPhones and I had none. He had plenty of old sickening patients to deal with and I had plenty of sickening girls to deal with.

I had aspirations not to become a doctor or engineer or lawyer or an aero-plane pilot or a banker or a business person. I wanted to be an author, sculptor, poet, musician or a singer or a painter. I wanted blonde hair, red neck, white face, black nails and a wide brain and a large heart, small stomach and twisted smile. I wanted to be an abuser to self, family, community and society. I wanted to abuse sun, moon, stars and the whole galaxy. I didn't want to be charming like my mother or workaholic like my father and rude like my sister.

I also didn't want to be news hungry or cuisine maker or party thrower or brooder like my grandparents. I wanted to be away from my tall angry Uncle or short laughing Aunt. I also wanted to be away from books unlike my, another Aunt or lanky bearded another Uncle. I didn't want to be a big fat hen or small thin squirrel. I didn't want bland diets and wanted junk food, so yummy and so tasty. I also didn't like pseudo-philosophical talks of my Guard, who is writing books which do not sell. I hated to go to his smoke laden stuffy room and sit with him to do home-work brought from school.

What was I supposed to do? I had a life of my own as I hear movie characters speak. I had a time span to spend, a career to make, a goal to be achieved and make myself happy. I was angry on the world to have dumped me in a backward country full of retarded and greedy people. Oh! Where did I land. I was narrating my incidence of birth. My seemingly careful Momma wanted to bring me to this world before time. She probably thought, as I have over heard that my birth would have brought some change in her conditions.

Guard visited thereafter and things were brought under control. We were left indoors while both parents worked outdoors. I was told my mother was a banker, then why she was not rich but did not deprive me of popsicles and loll-pops. My biological father worked on some menial job, return home late and watch movies on his laptop. My mother and Guard used to attend to household chores. Guard was a good cook but I did not like his delicacies. I had to swallow his preparations with gulps of water.

While strolling in the parking lot I was put down and took the first few steps to start walking. Since then I was always moving around. I would run to phone's shrilling tone, while Guard would waddle behind me to attend to calls. He helped my mother to fight for her rights, but he had to go back to retire from his government job. After he left my mother got her legal status and planned to visit her country of origin.

The oft repeated saying of my Momma about the phrase, that what goes around comes around, gripped my mind. I used to repeat it even when I was alone. I don't really understand it, but what my mother probably meant is people get the life they deserve, but it didn't suit me. I did not deserve what I was getting. Guard used to say, people get the treatment they deserve. It was pathological, another word commonly used by him. Guard was a doctor of no repute, struggling with competition and comparison. But was knowledgeable and hard working. But knowledgeable people need not work hard.

In Momma's opinion it is purchasing problems, in Grandma's opinion it is destiny, in Guard's own opinion it is the tests and trials of life and in my opinion, it is pure craziness. When I would ask him to open a hospital or clinic, he would say it is like opening a shop and waiting for customers to arrive, or when desperate praying for the clients to fall ill. And he was against making this honorable profession a business or industry. He would go to attend patients when called, those who need him and he would part with his advice to them. He would never collect money from patients directly, it is always reception mediated.

My Grandma was a hard worker too. She would get up very early, pray and worship first, then cook for the family, then clean up the mess and help me to get ready for school, walk up to the corner to let me board the bus, then she would arrange things, undertake pending assignments, sew some clothes, visit the neighbors, help the needy and make some snacks and lunch, wait for Guard to return, serve him food and accompany Guard for after-noon naps, to get up and get ready to go out shopping and comeback to participate in social activities and watch TV serials and sleep late to get up early.

While this was going around as a routine, my mother was pursuing her parent's American dream and returned back to struggle and to survive. I don't know for how long this continued. In spite of not having been born on streets, she was street smart and knew how to face and cope up with tasks big or small. She would not easily accept defeat. She would manage things somehow and used to visit me, while I was put to school. Not one but many, rather I was shifting schools. People say, it is a crisis event for children, but I never felt that away. I could interpret it as a welcome change and learning lessons.

All this was a fast-forward motion picture being seen in haste. I was a stubborn child having become immune to anything. I did not undergo crisis intervention, no stress busting, no crucial affairs to feel bad and no gross problems. Everything was accommodatable and no condition was challenging for me. My circumstances were balanced with minimum outside help. I was sailing smoothly, only occasionally I would throw temper tantrums but that was normal, Guard assured me. I would be naughty at times and sober at other times.

When I was learning history lessons, they denoted a different picture. I learned that all the great empires from history like Roman, Egyptian, Indian and Mongolian and background of civilizations like ancient Greek, Babylonians, Indus valley, roman and Persian all bloomed in temperate climates or tropical climates. None of the great empress were established in cold climates like in America, Russia, Canada and British common wealth. No doubt they spread to colonize the word as parasites and dictated their tactics and cunningness but confined to pleasant climates.

I hate the climate of mid-west, where people say that they are blessed with four seasons. Four seasons which are never on time, Guard would say three seasons only, and describe them as 2 months on white season, followed by 6 months of gray seasons, stretched before and after white, followed by 4 months of multicolor, including green and yellow and red. I would have preferred a month of violet too. He hated the culture and the busy schedules of life, when every one seems to be running behind one thing or the other. Guard would try to crack funny jokes, maybe funny in his books but not funny to me.

I forgot to tell you one incident. I used to find faults with him, but he used to take them sportively. He said that I shouldn't try to be his mother. I found that an interesting title given to not even a teen ager. And since then he started calling me Mom. Once he narrated an incident of his friend by name 'Ginger-claws', in short form GC who he told me had less income and more children. More than necessary was his opinion. He started narrating his friends short stories to me. who always was making a wit and humor out of himself. The way Guard used to describe in the manner of speech that I would know what was going in his mind.

Once I was made to believe, his friend was sitting in the hall after returning from his office and after removing his coat, underneath which there is a skin-tight T shirt, which would highlight his lean thin bony structure, with rib cage to count the number of ribs. His house was poverty stricken with no back yard or even a back door. He saw a stranger passing the hall holding a polythene carry bag, crossing the by-lane. He stopped him to enquire who he was and he was told that he is in a hurry to get some vegetables from the market. Then he was enquired why is he crossing the hall and the reply came as, making a short cut. Guard stopped. I expected the story to continue, but that was all.

I couldn't understand and I said what is this story, a comical one or a tragic one. He said comical. The he laughed an infective laughter and we both laughed aloud. Guard would narrate jokes in such a serious way that it would appear as though he has just returned from a funeral ceremony of one of his friends. But that is the way it went. That is the way it always used to go. Guard himself should have been in a situation like his friend then he would have realized whether it becomes a comedy or tragedy.

I was telling about American dream and the efforts I was expected to take being an American citizen, who was temporarily placed in the sub-continent. I was expected to be raised in eastern traditional way to become a useful citizen of the west. I was like a caterpillar to come out of the cone to turn into a butterfly and fly high. Adjust in the west and prove my worth. In the east it was called a land of opportunities, with freedom of speech, freedom from racial discrimination, etc., etc. I have to see and analyze and then comment. Till then no comments.

West had a different slang of English and difficult for me to understand initially. The system of coaching almost incomprehensible for me. Math, was in plenty and projects given to kids beyond their capacity to perform. Grades were also named different and discipline more than required, but one gets used to such things and time passed by and life lived by, as conveniently as possible for a girl of my age subjected to such drastic changes. Guard would describe it as tests and trials of everybody to face and stand them. Easily said than done.

There had been a clear demarcation of my stay in the east and the west. First 2 ½ years I lived in the west, following 2 ½ years in sub-continent and thereafter another 2 ½ years in the west and yet another 2 ½ years in the west and thereafter continued and still here. Elders take decisions and youngsters have to face the consequences. Of late I was taught the 1st and 2nd amendments of our constitution and felt not all are following it. I myself felt sideway glances of discrimination from the student community. Children learn from the parents, Guard always used to say. I didn't like it. Teachers were occupied by enough work load to give attention to these small deviations.

In the east I was put to the nearest private school after being shifted from another private school and it was walking distance. Initially Guard used to drop me and used to pick me, later I started going and coming back on my own. We were living in a bungalow with duplex building and were placed very comfortably. The view of the fort and the tombs was getting obstructed by rising multistoried buildings, more over it was always great to appreciate scenes for few days then it becomes a routine and I stopped enjoying it. There were cast iron gates and my Grandma would formally be there peeping out of the gate to greet me.

The small dwellings turned into school had small classes with no fans and the compound wall was decorated with cartoon paintings, of Donald duck, Mickey mouse, etc. so ugly looking that I would have preferred grave yards and cemeteries instead. The school bell was manually rung and we used to rush out to return home. Guard would be waiting for me to be picked up, and we would take few stopovers for sandwiches, ice creams cones or bars and occasional chips and candies. All those recollections were fun. I was getting acclimatized to the schedule.

There erected a huge building tall just in front of our house. But there was no lift provision and the principal used to remain from early morning to late evening and there was a fearful atmosphere prevailed during her presence. Why does she have to spend so much time in school. She must be a disordered person who does not find peace at home. Guard could have treated her better and relieved her of her ailments.

Then I was put to another private school having fans and water coolers, curtain hanging to cool off the hot winds and kids were more well behaved. Teachers were well mannered and the class rooms well lit. I was given less home-work and more time to play. There were wooden swings and slopes to slid down and a collections of flower pots to exhibit like a small garden in ne corner. I used to carry tiffin boxes for lunch and eat on the stairs swallowing cold food with water bottle gulps. I could have survived even otherwise.

I was then recommended to yet another better private school, with wide courtyards, play grounds and swimming pools plus running tracks. I was given admission and the surroundings were elegant and teachers politer. The rich class could have afforded the fee and kids were brought by private cars. I used to ride school bus but was happy anyway. I had a red plastic car to peddle by feet to move about in any available space and enjoy as though driving my own car.

Then came a big change in my schooling career. My elders spoke to some acquaintances visiting US, who were running a big school in our home town and managed to get me admitted. It was a big school, with big green lawns, big play grounds, big swimming pool, big class rooms, big staff, big gate and everything big. It was a big organization and big shot children were admitted to it. It was placed in a sub-urban locality called big city and there was a big distance from home and big busses used to pick children from all over the twin cities, the number of which were also becoming bigger by passage of time.

The place was airy, rather windy and teachers were airy too. For fear of being fired they were trying their hard to pretend as surrogate mothers and were trying their best to be sweet and affectionate towards students. Lunch was served and snacks were served and studies were served and games were served and juices were served. Of course, that did not make any difference but as I was to travel in a school-bus, I had company of boys and girls from my locality with whom I got friendly and I was having good time.

The school claimed to be teaching the prescribed syllabus of US public schools. I was getting adjusted to this change too. Guard's research institute where he used to part lectures was on the way and he used to visit me often. I heard that my mother's mother-in-law had arranged the wedding of the administrators and they were being considerate to me. Numbers were not given against the test performances, instead they used to label, exceeding, competing, compensating and things like that.

My association with the administrator spread as breaking news and I was given some relative importance. In sub-continent links and contacts have their advantages. I started learning swimming, musical instruments, dancing, ground skating, not ice skating and I started with my running practice and I ran fast, fast enough to win prizes. I was declared a 'wonderful helper'. Out of my habit of pleasing others. All were happy with me. I was happy writing essays and eating delicious south Asian cuisines. I hope I will be nominated for next Olympics for junior child category.

The food was served in metallic plates by black maid servants, while the cook or chef would be eating in some remote corner. There were less students admitted that year and there was no paucity of space to eat. We could have selected our own spaces, preferably corners to assemble and eat and pass on remarks on the tastes of cuisines. We could as well have been lying down and eating if need arise or if we wanted to venture in adventure. There was freedom of movement and freedom of selections.

The change also was the numbering of the buses, my bus was numbered 19 when there were altogether only 10. They must have wanted to impress about the count, like big hotels number their rooms from 100 onwards, to make believe that the hotel occupies so many rooms. Probably it pleases them, so let them be pleased. Sometimes my Grandma would walk me to the street and send me off the bus, sometimes servant maids would replace her and in emergency Guard was available.

Very occasionally there would be no one to collect me on return trip, and I used to be reluctant to get down and cross the street on my own. Once the driver urged me to get down, as he had several stops to make and in that process the school bus maid slammed the door so fast that my fingers were caught in the bus door and started bleeding. I cried and every one was harassed. They suspected fractures and pleading totally guilty brought me to our house. Seeing the blood draining from my fingers, my Grandma started crying too.

I had to console her and Guard carried me to his friend pediatrician and I was dressed by creams and bandages. He announced no fractures, which a relief to Grandma, more than me. But she was still crying and I also started crying and the trainee nurses started crying and it appeared a scene of mourning than a mere petty accident. Guard passed a gesture for me to behave bravely and I did. He smiled and I smiled too. We returned home but not before I was given a bag full of medicines.

I hated medicines for their bitter taste and untimely swallowing, mostly after food. I was given some juices to wash off the taste. Neighbors and relatives gathered and I go some attention, which curiously I enjoyed. I wished there must be occasional accidents happening once a year, for want of so much attention. They brought fruits and biscuits and chips and carbonated drinks of my choice. It turned to be fun without pain. When my Aunt returned from her college she almost threw a fit, she as sobbing or laughing I couldn't differentiate, but everything was brought under control.

Except that she wiped her eyes and nose with her books. She was a lover of books. She was always seen reading course books and would sleep with books, and if allowed would dress herself with books and may even eat books. She had load of books, which a donkey may be reluctant to carry on its back. She made books as pets, other than cats which were her weakness. She had funny named cats, like 'Chancha', 'Loveleta', 'Surmi' and 'Papchi'. She was very fond of them and would hug them first on arrival at home. I would have preferred names like sapphire, ruby, emerald, gold and silver.

She was herself very pretty like a jewel in the crown and was even declared Miss. University once. But she was modest person and never boasted high of herself. Only if she gets annoyed her face become longer and gruesome. But she had a sense of dressing and if my mother could have become Miss. World, she would certainly would have become Miss. South Asia or Miss. Asia Pacific. She was brown but brown is a better color than black. I like to be white, as they are a beauty and I was an ugly duckling. White is a sober color but brown is haggard, white is celebrated but brown is defamed. But life had to be lived on, plus Guard's corrective advice that what ever may be the color, confidence is a pre-requisite of success.

Guard could justify anything, he would have a ready-made answer for any situation, of course to justify. He would say, 'Mom, you are a contrast and you know something, contrasts stand tall and recognizable among the matches'. He would continue, 'Mom, you have an individuality which others are deprived of, so be happy with what you have'. What an explanation, what a consolation and what a paradigm. A word I have just learnt during an online project.

Wait. I was telling you about my new school. I had to carry less books, my backpack became very light, almost empty with out junk food and water bottle. I was light weight myself, as though a free bird, free to fly as I liked flying, if not myself at least kites. In this season Guard would get a lot of kites and thread, to fly kites and he was perfect in flying kites and would wage wars with other kite flyers. He would ask me to hold the kite which would rotate on its own, but Guard would claim he has asked the kite to do it for free, as though he has ordered somersaulting in the sky. He wanted children to become independent, as per his explanation of child psychology knowledge.

I used to sleep in between my grand-parents, vertically to begin with and later would find myself lying horizontally, pushing both of them at the brim of the bed, my head in grand-mother's bulging belly and my feet on the face of Guard. But they never minded and would adjust them selves by turning the other way. We had to adjust all at the same time, as the room could not occupy any more bed. As such my age to sleep separately was fast approaching. I was gradually shifted to the ante-room and Guard used to remain story telling until I fall sleep and next morning they would find me in their bed. But with time I adjusted to this arrangement and was sleeping independently and was proud about it.

Curiously what helped me was the background noise of Grandma watching the TV serials in local dialect of stories of rows between mother-in-law and daughter-in-law, all hateful but she was addicted to them and couldn't sleep without watching few serials. I think Guard should have kept some clear lines of his tricks about psychological treatments for himself or his wife, who would sleep at anytime she likes under the quilt with no hesitation to snore. But I think he was also used to them and found some relief in it. Somehow Guard succeeded in letting me feel secure while sleeping alone in my room now stuffed with soft toys. He said he has used the gradual withdrawal method to help me feel independent. It is difficult to understand his logic at times.

I used to get up late in the mornings until water is sprinkled on my face and I would throw some temper tantrums before fully waking up. I would eat breakfast with disinterest and would swallow boluses of eatables thrusted in my mouth, while Guard would help me wearing socks and shoes and putting my backpack and shove me out to be able to catch the bus in time, but not before he would tie a ribbon, some pins and some kind of belt to match the uniform, which was not at all required. The bus horn would be heard while I was stepping out of the gate and the driver could see us approaching. When I return all the gadgets would be removed one after the other and I was refreshed by cool shower given by Grandma.

I was given the award of fastest runner in relay races and individual rounds. I was a fast runner. I would run for my life as though to escape from a monster. The awards were plastic colored golden brown with colorful ribbons to be garlanded. Talking about golden brown plastic medals, I was reminded of my brown Uncle. What a tall handsome man he turned out to be. Sharp featured and serious faced bespectacled with grim looks. I had hardly seen him smiling or laughing except once or twice in company of his friends. He was a late sleeper and a late riser. He would not spend time indoors and mostly seen outdoors. He had plenty of friends and all were fond of him. He could make and sustain friendships.

One of his friends was very short and two of them would closely mimic a scene from Laurel and Hardy movie and he would maintain the trends of the fashion. He was a lavish spender. He was popular among the people in restaurants and market for his tipping. He would give tips to vendors, gas station fillers, taxi drivers and auto-rickshaw sitters. Some time he would give tips to Grandma and me as well. Anything was fine with me. I was afraid he may do the same to Guard some-day. He would try hard to avoid his father and Guard for some unexplained and un-complained reasons. May be the activities he was involved in spending Guard's money, which makes him little cautious.

He would bring all of my favorite toys, candies, junk food either under influence of his mother but he himself used to like them and want to share it with me. He would play with me hide and seek, air lifting me, pretentious boxing, wrestling games and what not. He was a kind person. I was made the bride maid to his bride from NZ. His bride was a total contrast to him. He was serious and she was hilarious, he was tall and she was short, he was brown and she was white, he was cool even if he is anxious inside and his wife would be always moving and calm and controlled. I wondered why such contrasts were brought together. Both were contrasts to their last match.

She would be awaiting a chance to laugh and he would be awaiting a chance to be grim. She could resist everything except laughing impulsively or against it. But she was a pleasant natured person and girlish in all respects. If I like a teddy bear she would want it as badly as I can, if I like a gaudy frock she would also want the similar type and if I like to wear jewelry she would do the same. She was an interesting character. She had a slang to English which only NZ people could understand, but she knew local dialect too which she would attempt speaking with elders.

My Grandma and she were best friends. They were seen chatting together, gossiping, at all times, even after she left to NZ they would resort to the same on phone. I sometime see her chatting with her mother-in-law, that is my Grandma while I was going to school and found continuing the dialogue as I return. How much of small talk content they both could share, was an element of surprise in itself. It is not serious discussion or some grave problem they would be discussing and it is always the ladies small talk, not back-biting. Thank God.

Oh! My disjointed thoughts. They drift here and there, come and go. I forgot to tell you that why Guard tries to stand when his son appears. He replied by saying 'Out of respect to his physique, he being tall and wide, muscularly built and also of course to bring some humor to the life'. He did not realize hat his humor may be budding some inhibitions in his son to start avoiding him. Guard's elder brother on the other hand was our neighbor and whom all of the youngsters called 'Big Pepa' and he looked like 'Daddy Pepa'. Big, fat, white and jocular. They used to drop at our place any time without notice. Our doors were always open for them. His wife was a witty person and they used to exchange jocular comments to each in private or in public.

She was fond of ice creams, bars or cones. Big Pepa used to bring a lot of ice creams flavors and she would eat them indiscriminately. Both of them were affluent at their bellies and may appear like penguins from a distance. He had a type of wit in his description of stories, but he has to get into mood for that. He will get into mood when there is audience of his type, otherwise he would decline the requests. He was good in mimicry too. There is lot which he narrated and narrated repeatedly and all enjoyed his talks, including me.

The story was about the floods which came to old city, after heavy rains and the river separating the old city with the new city was overflown and the details, Big Peppa would avoid about the catastrophe which took place then but used to narrate the incidents which followed thereafter. Some time later people had not completely forgotten the hazards of the so, called floods. Then spread rumors that floods are coming again and are already on the way. Very much there almost reaching and 'floods coming'. It was actually a rumor but people started reacting differently.

I was told that great grandmother and another Uncle were out then on some shopping spree and on hearing the news decided to return home. No conveyance was available as all were running everywhere to save their lives. No one was willing to face the coming floods. They walked home, quite some distance making their way among the troubled people like troubled waters. People running everywhere but reaching nowhere. Great grandmother held that Uncle's hand so tightly that the marks remained for days to come.

I believe the family residence was on the second floor and every neighbor, every relative and every friend, found the second floor a rescue place for shelter. The building did not collapse but shaken a bit by the number of people who occupied it at that time. Guard was at the gate watching the madness around, the they moved towards the main street. Guard's elder cousin sister saw these friends moving out and enquired in which direction they have gone. Someone said to the left and she fainted before shouting that he went towards the 'coming floods'.

Some distant relatives sister-in-law who was a teacher ran into the house carrying the starched saree for the next day school duty. Big Peppa will never stop when he has captured the interest of the audience. Some neighbor returned from office and knocked at the house door. Upon enquiry as to who is around, he in a confused state of mind uttered the word 'floods' and inside everybody started jumping on beds, tables, stools and chairs and trunks. He wanted to emphasize the fear laden minds of insiders even on hearing the house owners voice.

He narrated that in one of the wedding ceremonies when groom heard about the floods, he started running, held back by the would-be father-in-law and requested to carry the bride, he meant the rituals could be undertaken later. There were band instruments players running spontaneously and upon reflex one was pounding on his drum with regular intervals and the trumpet players concorded with the rhythm subconsciously. The usual wedding folk songs they are habituated to play.

There was a nearby hill station and all the grooms were accumulated by taxi drivers on the top, some with their brides and some alone, having been charged the fare at the ratio od 1:10. After some time the hill was cramped by garlanded grooms and taxis, with no place for private cars loaded with families and children. He would shift his narration to typical garlanding ceremonies of functions, a tradition where women folk will be eager to garland the couples and also want to be photographed or appear in front of videographer and in doing so with their broad bases would almost hide the bride and the groom, whose close ups would show only bases of fat ladies, half recumbent on themselves.

He would practically demonstrate the show and all would laugh out aloud. It was lot of fun of such dramas enacted in our living room. Guard was comparatively different. He would be humble and pretend to be poverty-stricken war veteran having led his own gallantry and he would have his own critical remedies for all his observations. Favors were asked for his wife and not for himself. He seems to be far beyond asking favors. My brown Grandma and Guard were exemplary couple with a façade of secrets. No one would know, who is the abused.

Such things are seen in articles of school magazine when some fool hardy writer would write about who's who and leave the readers to visualize the victim. Well those are stories about the school but I was talking about the stories of home. My Grandma always craved for attention. She was already getting attention from Guard, from outsiders, young or old males or females. She was crazy about new dresses. I had never seen her wearing the same dress twice. How she manages was a different story. No doubt she looked great in all costumes, branded, hand stitched, tailor made or designers. She had an appeal on every dress she wears.

This does not get restricted to dresses, they also included the artifacts of other accessories of beauty. She was beautiful in her own way. Some brownish beauties have won awards in Peugeots' before racism started or fascism discovered or Nazism extinguished. She did not know much of the details of the backgrounds of the history. She knew how to get attention. One must have shifting complaints from chest pain, to giddiness, to jelly legs, to bad dreams, to heart burn, to burning urine and stomach cramps with no visible signs. There were many decorations to her medical files and Guard's friend doctors were aware of them.

Guard would refer her to his colleagues to listen to her complaints give some reassurances and advice to socialize, preferably to visit 'Lord Bazar', a famous old city ladies fancy shopping center. As she would not miss any wedding or party but doctors would also emphasize her to continue distracting herself from these non-existent or unimportant complaints. A heart doctor referred her to cinemas, a skin doctor referred her to swimming and sun bathing. A bone doctor referred her to jogging, cycling and Yoga. A general doctor has referred her to be photographed with closeups and preferably with celebrities.

On one Sunday morning, it was drizzling and all walls were wet and Guard called a friend living across the street to infuse her favorite glucose infusion. The young doctor complied to the request and visited us with the appliances, but when he rang the bell the infused water in the wall had already trickled into the circuit and he perceived a shock and fell down on the slope of the gate outside. All of us brought him inside and the same glucose drip was given to him and he also felt better. The young doctor's wife was watching the scene from her kitchen and came to thank us for having taken care of her husband.

So, where were we. Yes, we were discussing the neighbors. They used to visit our house exchanging bowls of curries, little from their sides and much from our side. Their servings were worthy of feeding my pet cat, but I had to resist the urge and let Grandma decide what she wanted to do with it. Guard narrated his friend, Ginger claw's (GC's) incident that he used to send one of the sons to the neighbor's house to ask for a bowl of lentil soup by saying that this bowl including it would be 13 bowls and that he would return on all counts after 1st of next month.

'Are you sure', I interrupted.

'Damn sure', was his reply.

'Tragedy or comedy'.

'Comedy', and we used laugh at it.

Big Pepa was crazy of tasty cuisines. He would like fried mutton or chicken or egg and would ask Grandma to make for him. He would finish all at our dining table. He was advised less oil or no oil, because of his obesity and high blood pressure. He was fond of me and would become a horse to ride me around on his back. He would crawl on the carpet because of his joint pains, but it was fun for me. They had three sons, all grown up and would occasionally visit us to sit on the edge of the sofa and vanish in no time. They would always carry combs in their pockets instead of pens and groom their hair more often than necessary.

There was a partition separating the front balcony and a partition separating the backyard. Our portion of the duplex house was cleaner, more attractive with paintings of Guard hanging on the walls and flower pots selected by Grandma and kept in the corners. My Grandma had a sort of abnormal attachment with me, having been beside from my birth till now, except occasional absentees. But we used to have arguments, rows, quarrels and battles, a kind of cat and mouse relationship but she was always concerned about my weight and would like to overfeed me. I lived with whites and browns and blacks at times similar to our house's interior decorations.

Guard was a funny creature, rather a full fledged certified comedian, as far as I was concerned. He was full of events of his friend Ginger claws, and he said one day when his friend returned from office, his wife noticed absence of tiffin carrier and shouted about having lost it. He replied with irritable voice that she is shouting as if she used to give him tiffin full of delicacies. He would retort by saying that he just used to carry the tiffin carrier to impress the people, but it used to be empty all the times.

What was missing was a circus arena and his white chalk painted face with a red colored rubber ball on the tip of his nose, otherwise he was a joker in his own right.

'Yes, what happened thereafter', I enquired.

'Nothing'.

'That's all'.

'That's all'.

'Comedy or tragedy'.

'Comedy'.

Then we would burst out laughing. He would suddenly stop laughing and I would have to do the same and then he would start again and I had to do the same, it used to continue until both of us were exhausted.

At other times he would be seriously preoccupied in thinking something and he would not even hear me calling first and then screaming and he would pretend dozing off and even pretending to lose his balance as if he would slip on the carpet. But all of it was for my entertainment and I knew it.

I was recollecting the past days of the past times, I had spent with Guard. We used to take turns to boss around with each other. But mostly I would ask him to do this and not to do that and he would quietly used to comply, but at the same time making faces of annoyance, which I knew were fake. He was justifying my title of 'Mom'. I used to behave like one and would ask him to do additions, subtractions with out putting them on paper and would ask spellings of words, which he would strain his memory to recall and verbalize properly keeping him on Guard. His replies were Guarded too.

He was a smart old man to yield to my orders in totality, as he knew I am also learning with him. Mostly these exercises were based on the prevailing moods and prevailing circumstances. He would pop up with an incident of his friend GC, we started calling now. Once I believe the hefty milk man arrived at GC's door and knocked hard. The inmates knew his manner of approach and kept quite inside. Open the door he knocked very hard, then his wife told him to open it, before he breaks open the door but he said, if he does it then the milk man will break open his head.

One decent neighbor of another faith heard the noises and intervened to know that GC had overdue payments and the milkman was bent upon collecting it. The neighbor managed to pay his pending bill and GC announced his thanks and added please keep visiting us in such times and the neighbor was amazed and stepped down. Guard stopped again and I asked was it a routine and Guard' reply was, every month's routine. I couldn't understand the system and the interactions, but such things were a common place with families of many children.

'Is it humor or sarcasm', I was inquisitive.

'Humor'.

Then I was relieved and we laughed together and enjoyed the scene. Recollections of those events used to make me laugh at school and teacher may even suspect that I had gone insane laughing to myself. But those were joyous days of our togetherness and I enjoyed the time spent with them. Memories crop up to my mind's surface often and I would record the events on anything around, paper napkin, piece of paper, calendar margins wherever I could endorse, to let me include in my book which I so intensely desired.

I recollected once I got stuck with my head in the railings of our stairs and couldn't bring it out. I don't know how I inserted it and where it got stuck. I shouted for help and

Guard was not around and my Grandma got harassed. She tried different positions with no avail. My aunt was applying oil thinking that it would lubricate the iron bars and let my head come out, but she failed. Every one around was trying different postures and different positions. Guard came in the end and pulled me out from the other side of bars with my body sideways and every one took a sigh of relief.

I vividly remembered the time of my toilet training, for which I was gifted a red colored pot, which made the training even more difficult and I would strain to get more stuck and Guard advised me to remain relaxed and to take time, as it is a natural process which would take its time and, in the end, I would learn. He proved right and soon I was rid of that red colored pot. It saved me a lot of embarrassment to embark on the red pot in front of servant maids and they seem not to mind because every child has to go through these maneuvers.

One day it so happened that I was watching 'Orji and cockroach' cartoon and Guard sat beside me looking at the TV screen. But I knew he must be thinking something else, maybe about my carrier and future prospects, or about my life. When the cartoon ended, I asked him 'How was it'.

'Good', was his laconic reply.

'Good? but did you like it', I asked.

'Yes of course, but it reminded me of another story of cockroaches, who assembled one day, a kind of re-union after a long time and were exchanging pleasantries. One of them boasted that he moved into a lavish accommodation, with clean living room decorated with antiques, nice kitchen with all electronic gadgets, cozy velvety bedrooms with beautiful curtain and a clean bath room shining with glazed tiles and fragrant attachments and......', but he had to stop his narration because all shouted at him by saying that they are getting nauseated. Guard stopped too. 'Then', was my question. 'That's all. The story ends here'.

'Comedy or tragedy',

'Tragedy', he made grumpy face and we all laughed. Later I understood that cleanliness is against the survival of cockroaches. Everything in my life went smoothly. Guard has a talent of converting comical stories into tragedies and vice versa. What a comedian he was. He could hide his tears by laughing and hide his pleasure by become cry some or serious. He should have been a joker in a circus. But he used to entertain the family and friends only and with strangers he was always reserved. I respected his personality and also his physical disability. He would be getting worried about the hardships, tasks, trials but he would avoid showing them. He would keep things to himself.

I lived with Guard's silences, Grandma's spices, Momma's attires, Dad's computer engrossments and my sister's notoriety. Things which I couldn't have helped. I didn't know I am misunderstanding them or they are misunderstanding me. I was becoming selfish. One has to be little selfish for survival, used to be Guard's notation. But each one has their own likes and dislikes, their own ways of passing time, their own preferences and gratifications. 'Think tall but remain small, dream big but remain humble', was another Guard's notation. He wouldn't stop at that. 'And little bit of anxiety is good for health'. I think he invents such remarks by himself.

One day I asked him, 'Do you like America'.
'No, I can't'.
'Why'. I asked.
'Because there every one is in a hurry'.
'So, what'?

He narrated 'Once there was a sub-ordinate walking briskly to his office on a pedestrian walkway of a bridge and his boss called for a lift in his car, to which he responded, No, thank you I am in a hurry'.

'What was that, a story, a joke or what'?

He smiled and said 'A joke'. And we laughed at it.

One day a servant maid's girl with clean shaven head came and I teased by paving my hand and she cried. I laughed to recollect the event when my head was shaved, and she stopped crying and looked at me amazed. Yes, it was an event to be recollected. Several shifts of school, tropical climate and girls keeping long hair was sure to get infested with lice and Grandma, as though waiting for this chance announced that my head will be shaved. She called a barber at home and he was enthusiastic to collect a tip and enquired from which side to start, right or left. It may be an omen but I was annoyed and told him start from north and turn west and then ……………… everybody laughed except me and I made a big fuss.

By chance a lady relative visited us that time she pacified the scene by cajoling me and the drama was over. It was summer time and I felt light headed. Then Guard applied a cool wet towel with his after-shave lotion over my head and it gave a nice feeling with a fragrance which I also liked. After few days my hair started growing and they were soft and Guard used to pass on his head and used to enjoy the bristles feeling. I hated to see my reflection in the mirror. I would turn back to check if it is someone else is behind me. This time I was given a red cap to wear. I was shy to go to school, but I went and found several other girls with shaven heads which was routine in summers and I felt a lot better, as no body cared about it.

I didn't want to remember another incident but couldn't help and thought how I had heat stroke or something and fainted. I was carried to my Doctor, who was black, short, bearded and bespectacled and he checked me and applied infusion and gave me some tasty syrups. When he palpated my stomach, I giggled and he was surprised. He could have easily mistaken to be a priest if his stethoscope is replaced by a cap. But he was a good Doctor and a kind man. I was hospitalized and again all trainee nurses were gathered around me with curious eyes and helped me to settled down. The appliances attached to me warranted an additional wire to be put into a socket to make me almost like a robot to do mechanical jobs.

I was compensated by my choice of drinks, juices, coconut water, biscuits, ice creams and toys, including a barbie doll wearing a Doctor's uniform. I could hear other kids crying and I imagined they are being given injections, but thanks God, Guard checked me and shortened the stay in hospital and we went home. The fear of hospitals was wearing off, rather I started liking hospital visits. I was given few days of rest and few days of relief from home work assignments, all very welcoming, including short stories of the Guard.

He narrated his friend GC's case, when his father-in-law visited his house unexpectedly and told that last time when his daughter, GC's wife gave him milk with think layer of cream and when he went home, he had stomach ache and vomited and found this thin white cap belonging to GC. GC was looking at the old man with amused looks, and he said to his wife give him another glass of milk, because since few days he is not finding his white thin T shirt. Guard stopped abruptly and my stare was questioning. 'That's all'. He said.

I asked him whether it was sarcasm or truth. He said sarcasm and we laughed for some time.

'You know something, Mom, kids cry before injections and not later'.

'Why'?

'Because the needles for kids are so thin that they hardly feel the pinch, but they cry for the fear of it, and when the needle is withdrawn they don't feel any pain and the injections are followed by cuddles and hugs. And when we were trainees in out patient departments, there used to be big queues of patients asking for white or yellow injections. We would have to hurry to complete the numbers and there were times when patients brought back the needles and told us that we withdrew the syringe but left the needle.

'Oh!', I was shocked.

'No, it was a routine in those days', he would console.

'And you know once, even after the injection was given the child cried louder and louder. The Doctor was surprised, from the gestures by his hand, he enquired as to why. The child said, that he will stop crying if the Doctor step away from his toes'.

'Then what'?

'Nothing'. Then it was Doctor's turn to cry because the angry boy whose toes were being crushed by the heavy weight Doctor, when the boy bit his hand and ran away'. 'Really'?

'Really'.

'True or false'

'False', then we laughed and laughed.

Time passed quickly. I was kept busy by 6 days a week school. Saturdays were half days but a lot of home work to be done. We helped each other and remained happy. The time when I would be doing my homework, 'Chancha' our pet cat would be brushing his tail or rubbing his head over my feet, as though I am a deity and he is a worshipper and I used to lift him in my lap and caress his head he would thank me by purring.

Once while he was crossing the street he was hit by a motorbike and acquired a fracture of his leg. I was saddened. Poor cat was crying with pain. I felt bad as he was like a friend to me. We used to chase around and play hide and seek. There was no bleeding which meant no open wound, but he was crawling to move. My aunt carried him to a veterinary clinic, where they applied a cast and gave some medication and we brought him back. I gave a soft cushion for him to rest and he slept for some time.

Guard brought some tinned fish and gave it to grandma to feed him. He was looking at all the inmates for pity. When his time to attend the litter came he moved slowly and attended his needs in the litter box. Grandma appreciated him and I thought poor fellow he did not make a big deal of it. I would in his place may have done so. He obediently took his medication and food and recovered fast. Even before the cast was removed he was walking and even was attempting to play cat and mouse chase.

I felt cat's life is better because cats can go around and come around any time of day and night, they don't have to go to school and they don't have tests and exams. They don't have to do any drills or perform any goals. My life on the other hand appeared like a railway track where trains move about and sometime it looked like train itself which have to shift rails and change their directions, as per the signals and likes or dislikes of the operators.

Momma used to visit me often, bringing toys and chocolates and last time she brought the American doll. She was cute and bulky. My friends in the neighborhood gathered to see her. As a tradition their mothers sent sweets and we all shared them. I had tricycle and foot driven car which I used to drive wearing shoes. My hair grew up to shoulder length and I had to tie pony tails to keep them in order. Grandma used to make good pony tails by tying little high up and I used to be comfortable with it. My uncle used to bring lots of balloons and I liked to pin them and pop out with a noise. It felt good to be among so many caretakers.

Once when I got up on a Sunday morning my hair was bushy and grandma already had plans to apply oil and turn them into beads. I didn't like beads. I was about to make a fuss, when Guard narrated another story of his friend GC, whose friend visited him with his son and the boy halted at the door, reluctant to come in. His friend looked both ways and the son with his bushy overgrown hair was like a lion's mane and the boy was equally stunned by the gaze of the GC whose face was lean, thin and gray hound type. He wearing a central cap over his balding hair and looked menacingly harmful. His friend told his son to come in and that the inmate will not bite him like a dog.

'Come on, how can a friend call his old-time friend a dog', was my eager enquiry. I stubbornly asked him again.

'Mom, there are plenty of stray dogs here and one of them had once bitten the boy and he was afraid. So, to pacify him he had to rest assure the son that he will not bitten again.

'What about your friend GC, he did not mind it' I probed.

'No, he did not as he has other worries to discuss with his friend and wanted to squeeze some money from him.

'Is it true or false'.

'True'.

'I don't believe it'.

'I don't believe either'. But, again we laughed because I knew he has made up this story for the fun of it.

Guard had plenty of stories in stock. He would retrieve them at the appropriate times and would narrate mostly to me. He was good company. My birthday was celebrated, a cake was brought with my name and icing of flowers and tendrils. It looked good. Ribbons were hanged and decorations were complete. They inflated hundreds of balloons after I slept and when I woke up I was amidst an ocean of balloons of same color of light blue, as though it is an ocean and I am expected to swim through them. I liked it and enjoyed the ceremony. My friends were given triangular cone like caps to wear and all sang the happy birthday song. Cake was cut candle blown out, big chunks of cakes distributed and cool drinks served, photos taken and hugs and embraces continued and I got tired and slept.

Next day was even more fun when we competed to pop out the balloons and the maximum number popped was to be declared the winner. It looked as though purposefully Guard let me win over the reward. And I was happy still. Uncle brought the photos and we all exchanged them to see and to enjoy the function on celluloid. I looked pretty in a pink frock with frills and a golden belt and hair left on the shoulders to curl up and people called me a fairy.

I think God had a special plan for me, but I am one among many. I also have to plan for myself. I can't be a statue to be placed at a crossing in the east or in a museum in the west. I am in between east and west. Even the games of east and west are different. I feel good when I am invited to their game in east or in west. Games are games. Games are fun. The rules maybe different but the spirit is the same. I feel good when my friends and family care for me. I would like to be like Momma, witty, cheerful and pleasing and I like to be like Dad, smiling, composed and balanced. I have to be a special girl.

I started recollecting my memories since maybe I was 3 years or earlier or later. It is difficult to remember. Elders tell me when I was born I looked like my Momma, as I grew up I started changing. It shouldn't matter to me anymore, because I am what I have to be. I should not expose my feelings to Momma, because she would worry for me. But I want to have a special bond with her and want to care for her. I am happy with what I am and I would be in future as well.

I think people missed my condition when they called me a restless baby. I maybe restless for a short time with my destiny. But Guard says we make our own destiny, and I think he is referring to future, otherwise fates are destined, is my grandma's opinion. Different people have different opinions. I should form my own opinion. I heard somewhere destinies are unknown to people. It is unknown to me as well. Who could forecast future, except fortune tellers. But they always go wrong. I don't know why people are interested to know their future. They want to leave the past but they think they must know the future, No, they must focus on the present.

People are interesting characters. They ignore their duties and worry for the future. To me it looked like jig-saw puzzle, whose pieces I am not able to put together to like it. It become shapeless. But I can't give up. I can't be strong headed. I am just a kid. If Guard calls me mom that does not make me one. He used to call me the same when I was younger and he would call me the same when I am grown up. What a funny word, which can be stretched to any length of time.

I maybe laughing at times and I maybe crying at other times but only out of pain. I get angry but it also fades away fast. People cannot even notice it. Good thing I am in a society which is normal. I don't want to face realities, realities like ground realities, as Guard puts them. What is the need of ground realities? My brain is functioning, my body is functioning and I try to please everybody. People say children try to please when they are insecure, but I am secure. I can build my own house, I can make my own walk way. I can hold on to whatever comes my way and can progress. Progress to the heights of success and fame.

When I am at home, I X-ray things, my own stuff, which belongs to me. I see my album and try to recollect my past. But what would be the past of a young girl, it can only be future. I don't want to be special, there is nothing special in being a special. It is better to be ordinary like all and mix with them easily. I can try some extra-ordinary things. I also don't want to be difficult, like others. I don't want to claim wise while remaining a fool. I want to be as happy as my sister. There may not be any treatment of texture and color change. I want to be like dolphins, how they jump and dive. They are not afraid of strangers. They bring their noses to strangers, without hesitation. Unlike my house maid, who was a moron and hesitate to do anything.

My parents are considering what is important for me. They must be having some questions about my future. I wish they should have developed enough confidence in me to keep them at ease. Things are moving and I am making progress. I am not stationary like a statue. I want to experience new things. I want to participate in kids singing competition and I want to take part in kids dancing live shows. I want to hold large concerts, huge audiences to be my fans on social media networks. I want to become Malala. I should become a song like the south Indian song which became viral overnight. I am forgetting the name, but how does it matter.

I want to run in Olympics and ride a pony on hills. Horses gallop fast and make loud noises and stand on hind feet for no reason. I get such dreams. Guard said to dream big. I some time get funny thoughts and act equally funny. Once I got a call on Momma's phone and immediately I told the lady caller to try on week-ends. Week days Momma remains busy, she remains busy even on weak-ends but I just wanted these callers to be stopped disturbing Momma.

I like the designers who take brown models to fashion shows and design beautiful clothes. I don't like designers who are after white models and do not know any original designs and just copy from others and bring some small changes. But designers with white models are famous and successful. What a joke? What a priority? I like to attend fashion shows and see models cat-walking on the ramp. One model stumbled and fell down and I couldn't control my laughter. People stared at me and I stared back at them. There was no need to control the normal reactions.

I want to be more independent, not relying on Momma or Dad or grandma or Guard even. I want to venture into mountaineering and bungy jumping or surfing or hanging on giant wheels of amusement parks. I enjoyed my trip to Disney land. My Dad wanted to move to warmer climate but he couldn't for some reason. Mid-west is not bad. Snow fall is not bad. I can make snow man and put a candle as his nose. I want to throw snow balls at my sister. But when the chance comes I forget my winter rubber gloves and get restrained from doing it. I should be more organized.

I get itchy at times. Not itchy as itchy, but I want to scratch my head if I am wearing my winter cap and want to scratch my finger when I am wearing winter gloves. I enjoy cartoons as much as books. Books for children. I had finished quite a few and donated them to the friendship center library, for other kids to read. I get ideas and discus with Guard. He sometimes approves, sometimes disapprove. I think it depends on his mood. I want to become an optometrist, physiotherapist, psychotherapist, techno-therapist all at one time. But not faith healer or spiritual healer. They are a humbug. Unreal and of no use.

I have a lot to learn, but is it a moment too late? No, it can't be. As I have just started to learn. It looked as if I am in a triangle and me in the middle. The heat is in excess. The tropical climate and population in excess and I seem to be pushed to the edge. Amidst the crowd I could hardly get a breath of fresh air. This would go on until the train stops at some station. Standing still is worse than moving. I feel I am moving to the school for exams. Exams are scary.

Suddenly a ray of light lit my eyes. I focused. I saw an angel. But I think I was wrong, angels at this place, at this time. No, I must be mistaken. As much as I prefer fiction than documentary and books more than the internet. I always get late to school, even Guard is carrying me on his scooter or I am riding on the bus. People are obstacles. They are always crossing streets. Some for newspaper, some for coffee and some for ATM machine or for any other thing. People are always crossing, not on zebra crossing but anywhere.

Now and then a face appears and disappears. Who is this. Why his projections cross my eyesight so often. I don't belong to any missing person, neither I am in search of any. I always wanted to say something to that face, but I get lost among other faces. I could find the evitable without the inevitable search. Not easy to capture in my memory. It comes and it goes. I will not locate him in this universe, maybe in the after-life. I am not sure who he is. What I was sure of is I am a pretty little girl with curly hair, curls falling on my shoulder and swinging with my movements.

There will be a moment when life would change on its own. Rotate on its own axis. Images which seem to be inches away would be in another continent. History is repeating itself but every time it is little different. But history repeats itself. I would change with history. I have a million questions surfacing on my mind. I don't know. Some faces are encouraging, some faces are discouraging. Some are serious and some are smiling. I feel my mind will explode. The memories were flooding, surfacing and disappearing.

I am sure in future at some point I may understand the ambiguity. I will know for sure. But I didn't want to wait for the clock to take turns and turns to change pages of the calendar. I felt I am in a hurry to know the facts. And I am happy for God's blessings, happy for God's mercy. The reality of life. I am happy, my family is happy. We are blessed by God's kindness. God is merciful and beneficent. One God only, who should be praised and who should be thanked all the times.

I want every thing precious, gold, silver and diamonds. Nothing semi-precious as sold in 'Lord Bazar' of old city. I will have to hold on to my destiny. I can even swallow my destiny, if it comes to that. I also want animated cartoons to be included in my destiny to keep me amused, but only when I am not studying, I don't know why I wander in my thoughts. I imagine and fantasize and I will wind up or land up back at the same place. The place where I was born, where I belonged, from where I originated. My feelings get into random emotions. I don't get illusions, that is a plus point.

Once I got into Momma's parked car, in the portico with the keys, as though I intend to go on a long drive, closed the doors and played with the accessories and didn't know how to come out. I shouted but the doors were closed and my voice couldn't reach outdoors. I started banging the glass panels and, in the end, someone noticed some abnormal activity and came out and pulled me out. I promised myself not to venture such intentions of long drive again, unless some elders are around. The fault was of my Uncle, who at times used to let me sit on his lap and allow me to hold the steering and to pretend as if I am driving. Whose fault and who's suffering?

I sometimes think why I shouldn't buy a lottery ticket and suddenly get rich, not very rich but rich enough to get some attention, some recognition, some name and some fame. I believe rich people can see through their future and I also want to get ahead and go on and on. That was a good feeling, but why Guard says good is not good enough, good is never perfect. Good and bad always go hand in hand. There are good days and there are bad days. I sometimes fail to understand Guard's ideas. He talks what he finds it fit, whether it is meaningful or not.

I want persistent relationship, never ending relationships for me to get plenty of imaginations. Not temporary relationship or business relationship. My dreams should last forever and my rewards should last forever. I don't want to walk away when my dreams are getting me fruits, results and distinctions. I don't want secrets and I don't have any. I am an open book for anyone to see through. But in that case, I shouldn't be thinking at all. I should let things come and go as destined. It all seems so complicated and controversial.

People who meet on trains are strangers. But I cannot live a life like riding on trains with strangers. You can be strangers when you first meet, the you become friends and then you become family and living among family is the best. I could create myself from that background. I will not disappoint me or Momma or Dad, but I can disappoint Guard if not always at least sometimes. I will prefer truth and not lies. Lies cannot remain for long while truth can. It is easy to tell truth, because you have to narrate what has happened, but for lies you have to invent few, chose the best and tell and next time you may forget and tell a different story and in the end it is not easy. You may get caught easily.

I can search and find myself. I am not the type who don't want accidents. Accidents do take place and even miracles take place. My birth is a miracle. My presence in sub-continent is a miracle. Miracles can cause pain sometime, but pain is also necessary for life. Guard says pain directs out attention to take care of what is painful. Pain keeps memories alive. Pain can magnify memories to look through easily. I can sleep with my memories, even if they are shady and smoke laden, Unclear and blurred, but no harm. One can live with their memories, big or small, minute or magnified.

Let me be honest. I don't even remember the village where I was born. In the west they say suburb, but how does it matter. Even if I am carried there I may not recognize it, because the landscape must have changed. Big buildings must have been constructed on barren land. Economy grows and nations grow and children grow and they have to accept the changes. I will accept the changes.

Momma says when hardships fall on us, we should not feel bad, rather we should wait as hardships are always followed by relief. Relief is good. It was quotation of Holy book. Momma is a wise woman, and a brave one too. People say she has come out of impossible or next to impossible situations on her own. She has changed into a new person, she is not the same person, as she used to be. I will also be a new person like her. If not exactly like her at least similar to her.

She straightened her problems and came on track. Track of the righteous path, as described in Holy book. She would sure to become a celebrity one day. She tells me never become a victim of circumstances. She says it is important to keep promises. In Guard's opinion promises are assurances for convincing only. They should be given to you by yourself. You should promise and keep up to it. Kept promises keep everybody comfortable. I had had enough of his advices and I thought I better shift towards Grandma and pray with her, not alone but with her together.

Momma says that I should be stable, I should grow up. What exactly she meant was not easy to grasp. I wanted to tell her that she should not treat me like an infant, soon I am going to be a teenager. But what is the big deal to be a teenager. It is not a qualification for girls in America. Momma says that if I will be good girl I will be given a smart phone. I wanted to ask her when. I knew she would say when you become a good girl. Does she mean that I am not a good girl now? I think, she means, I should be a good girl always. I wanted to ask her for how long. But I didn't because she may not an answer to it.

I also wanted to ask her that she has a daughter and we should be together. Is it not a rule breaking idea for the norms of the family? There are commitments to be met. Commitment of living together, respecting each other's likes and dislikes. I think children should get into a contract with their parents to bind them, to give us the needed joys of life. I think these are times of trials for me. God should send me an angel for my company. I know, angels like children. I have seen them in many children's cartoons.

I think Momma has some problems to solve first, problems unknown to me.

Once she called me from US on phone and I enquired, is she okay.

She replied yes, why, what could be wrong with me. I said I was just asking.

She replied, do I think she is not okay. I gathered some courage and told her that she is not okay.

Why? was her single worded question. I said because she wants me to be straight, as though I am deviated. Some times we have to confront for our defense, was taught to me by Guard. Some time we have to make choices among so many and some time we have to be different than our usual self. But we have to take the right decision in the end.

World has two sides of understandings, like two sides of a coin. They will choose which one they like and that is the truth. I was aware of relations and their responsibilities. I am raised to be a good citizen and to be a peaceful co-inhabitant of the society and also respect the legacy of considerations. But how elders expect a child to play such hard roles. I would prefer lying dormant and to let things take their shape. I can't be a pendulum of a grandfather's clock.

Children also deserve a voice and a choice of their own. They should get both.

They can cheer as cheer leaders of some game. They should cheer in the name of peace and kindness. The status asked for, is for independence. There should not be any impediments, impediments become weaknesses, weakness become submission to wrong doings, and submission is a source of nutrient for abuse. I am not going to be abused. Abusers are fools of the highest degree, as they do not know how abuse can retort to stubbornness and rebellion.

Children need not be vulnerable to causes or effects, they need not be vulnerable to their primary or secondary needs and they need not be vulnerable to any other reason. To be vulnerable is violation of human rights, as I was taught in school. Elders are better placed but children are also given a lot of rights. A child is a state's property, I was told by a teacher. But in the pretext of understanding, I would prefer to remain a property of parents.

So, in America the popularly called rich country, where immigrants under some dreams are eager to come and try to live a miserable life, I was told. I have not seen any except locals who are homeless on streets. They beg in the day and sleep under the shelter of churches in the nights. What a pity? I think I should learn 'Karate' or some martial arts instead doing a degree in medicine or law. No one could help them. I could teach martial arts to homeless and let them live a life of dignity. They can show their tricks on the streets and earn a living. The moves are brisk and impressive and they keep people fit. Guard does not believe in expressing it that way. He says homeless people are sick people. Emotionally sick. But I think they have emotions.

I feel harassed by some homeless, I get tired at looking towards them. I sometimes get fed up seeing them at the crossings and in the parking lots. I think I should quit. I pity people who are deprived of home's comforts. I get lost if I get such thoughts. I always find difficult to judge people, judge their intentions and their smiles. It is not easy to know people. People blame each other. It is easier to blame others than to ourselves.

Guard had a different philosophy of life. Once I asked him, 'Why not you come to America'?

'I can't because I don't have children who are qualified nurses'.

'What is the connection'?

'Because, otherwise you will have to go to shelter home for the aged, as they have qualified nurses and they can take better care of old people'.

What a thought? A thought to be heard and erased. But he was serious and doesn't seem to be kidding. He always kids with me. He changed the subject because of the gravity of implications.

'And' he said 'if chances come in life, you should take them. You would be perfected by imperfections'. All that I could understand was nothing. Hopefully some time in future.

He would say, 'All needs are based on genes. Different people will have different needs because of different genes'.

I think he is not much aware of genes. He doesn't know the truth about genes or genetic loading. As far I had learned genes carry characteristics of parents or ancestors to children. I did not carry my parent's characteristics. No doubt, I was good looking, my teeth were perfect, my lips were perfect and my eyes were perfect, but I was lean and thin in spite of eating junk food and I was brown. But I carried the genes of Momma to please people, and of Dad that I try to help, my charging to help people leads to their irritation and I can not understand how I can help people and please them, to come under their good books if I am charging them.

Guard had an answer for that. 'Don't ever try to please people and more so all at one time, you can't and if you still try then you may make more enemies than friends'.

Oh! What a way to explain my failure. I think he was trying to please me.

He says, 'People will smile because they have expectations with them for satisfaction, but they don't know how, so they are left with the only option of smiling'.

I think I must not give much attention to his talks. He talks wisely at times and he talk foolishly at times. I must learn the teachings of Holy book and faith. But why do people change their faiths, was another question which used to haunt me often.

People become atheists when it comes to God and they become gods when it comes to their achievements, not knowing that achievements are blessings from God, as Guard always mention. People change their faiths and religions based on their needs not genes or better still for their benefits at any given time. What an irony of faiths? As though faith are false beliefs seeded by the parents. We can not see the God but we can for sure see the signs, that God exists and controls the universe. Leave alone the world. Kingdoms or senates. I know among different presidents of America some were democrats and some were republicans.

But I wanted to be sure whether I am right or wrong or the world is wrong or right. I am a girl not to be dominated but to be respected. I wanted to know everything right and wrong. People walk by laughing and giggling and I sit and watch them. Are they pretending to be happy but actually they are not, when I am sure I am happy I need not show off? I am going to create my own story and I am going to be part of my formed story, which may be a test. This point was still not clear in my mind. Stories are not eternities, so why to worry now. To write a story one has to be smart.

How do people become smart? Smart guys are born smart, here comes the roles of genes, I think. Smartness is gifted and some remain fools, trying to become smart and with passing time they convince themselves that they have become smart, when actually they remain fools. But smart people simply do not believe in people until they are sure about them. My problem is I believe in people, even when I suspect that they are trying to cheat or fool around. But when words are given they are meant to be believed.

Guard interferes everywhere, he says 'Mom, you just believe in yourself. Don't let others influence you, except your own self'. Its contradiction of what he taught me earlier. Here conflict of interests was involved.

Once I broke my glasses. Grandma took out the old prescription, took me to the nearest optician and let me select the frame and this time I selected red color. I was getting habituated to red color. Grandma paid the bill and next day collected the glasses. I wore it and I found there is something wrong with it. Guard took it again and found out that the lenses were correctly numbered and correctly prepared but the optician had fixed them on the wrong sides, from left to right. It was re-corrected and I was back to normal. Such hazards were a common place in sub-continent.

Guard narrated a story of his friend GC, when he was resting at home having taken a French leave, one person bespectacled and wearing very thick glasses, must have been placed wrongly like mine, entered his house. He was wearing shorts and a hat. He introduced himself as the teacher from school. GC immediately stopped him with a gesture of hand and said, 'Master children learn from teachers and not vice versa, you shouldn't be wearing shorts'.

The teacher did not mind it as he was looking for a chair to sit, which didn't exist. GC's wife thought teacher had come to collect fees.

She said, 'Master, our children's fee should be waived off, as they study well'.

'What', exclaimed the teacher, 'No, your children do not know English, Math or even can draw an owl's pic properly'.

GC got annoyed, he called his son and asked him about what teacher was saying about him and the child nodded his head in approval. 'Can't you see and draw', he was pointing towards teacher. I grasped the joke and laughed.

'Must be a joke', I affirmed.

'No, it is sarcasm'. He replied and we laughed a lot imagining the situation and the humor behind it.

Sometimes I can be wrong, but not always. There are different rights and different wrongs for different people. Some like short hair some like long hair and they consider them as right or wrong. Some wear pony tails and some prefer crop cuts, some prefer lose hair hanging and some want beads. There is no right way or wrong way. It is people's choice. I need not hate them or love them. They are just people living their own life styles, some ordinary some extra-ordinary. But nobody is perfect, I am not perfect too. Certain things are complicated like keeping to bonds, keeping to calls, keeping to promises.

People talk about harmonious living, they talk about restraining their urges. I don't want to give promises, as promises are kept not broken. Promises can be meant for good or bad, they are not always the same and they change according to conditions. My conditions cannot let me keep promises. Promises are asked by people who are afraid of their secrets getting revealed.

People linger with their fears and fear keep them straight, as long as secrets are not revealed. But I cannot teach elders. My peer group ridicule me that I don't have hobbies. They show their coins, they show their stamps, but I cannot show them the words imprinted in my memories and collecting those words is my hobby. I have to play with words and I have won hearts by words. Gifts cannot win hearts. Words combined I became a small poem.

Poems don't have ego problems. I am not obnoxious and I don't hurt others. I care for them, rather I want to please them. What else I can do? What else people want from me. I know multi-syllable words, even if I don't know their meanings. I will learn them slowly. What is the hurry? But words can disappoint people, pictures of the past can disappoint people. They see their reflections in the pictures, which they don't want.

There is something wrong about people. They are divided in sects, castes, creeds, faiths, religions, provinces and nations. Why can't they remain united as one species? They are one species. People should show admiration for my thoughts, my feelings and my honesty. They can't ignore me, leave alone neglecting me.

I don't have options. I don't know when I would get my choices. I need to chose my goals, my dreams, my plans, my career, my skills and my talent to be used for the benefit of society. As instructed by almighty. What I could see are faces, sad faces, worried, depressed, fearful and abused, tranquiller by drugs, grieved by their sickness. I don't want to look at them. I will close my eyes.

I am normal. I am good, but not in that sense. I am awful but awesomely good person. To be good to others is great. Other's opinion doesn't matter, even if they call you awful or awesome. These are words. Words motivate me. I write for myself. Writing satisfies me with inspiration, determination and devotion. Guard always uses these words.

He says, cuisines may not please people as much as words and he also warn that words could be permanently deceitful like blessing in disguise. I should stick to my words. Decent words. I should communicate properly. If I could do that then I could become an artist in my own capacity. I want to look out of ordinary, not extra ordinary, but just out of ordinary. It would elevate me and I could be grateful to nature. Nature controlled by some super natural power, some almighty force, God, which can make me a condensed moon light, a punctuation of an incomplete sentence, a doctrine and a philosophy.

I found it funny that the word 'Mayonnaise' came from France when a cook made a new sauce in the honor of some victory. And I was also told that 'Avocado' is a vulgar word, not to be uttered, so not to be eaten. I could continue with this war on wards but I wanted to be a literate, so I have to learn vocabulary. I think I should mix words, but words would remain important then pictures. To be clearer, a poem does not require pictures, otherwise it will become a caricature. Poem needs words and words have to be phrased to show some underlying message. Words are required for conversation, communication in prose, essays, novels, etc.

I was told that the initial language was picturesque, people have to draw pictures to describe feelings and it was called sign language, as was seen in caves and pyramids. I don't want to wage war against authors, publishers, editors, readers or viewers. I only want to energize my words to the readers of my story. And of course, I require words as necessity and good thing most of the languages have same original words which got mixed up with them. New words are coined and new phrases added.

That is why I miss my previous schools because I was greeted by genuine smiles and genuine appraisals, so had good times then. But nothing matters in the end.

Not even words or pictures, what remains in the interpretation. What mattered to me was what pleases me, what pleases the world and what pleases the God. What ultimately matters are the God's directives and I knew God is silently watching the games of diplomacies, aristocracies and autocracies. New words I had just learned. Momma says, I don't have all the time in the world to learn as I wish, I have to keep pace with the work load, but I think it is asking too much from me. I hate math and I can't help to mix numbers for which I need all the time in the world. I don't want to be surrounded by people who judge me and I may better remain unjudged.

This is not appropriate and I will not tolerate it. I have to be ready for wars and judgements too. How would they know that authors are more than words and artists are more than their paintings? I will review the points of judgement. Words I will stick with, as words are my treasure. I will keep them under lock and key. I will start writing in school magazines, as magazines are a reflection of school's standard. But administrators may not agree. Let them not. It should not matter to me.

My priority is to know my ancestry. My heritage, my origin, my difference of color. I want facts, not replies like 'You would know when you grow up'. Or answers like 'People who don't get along have to find their own ways'. How people don't get along, as to get along is to make small compromises. I also don't get along with people at times. At time I like people and at times I dislike the same people. I am old enough. My parents tell me I am old enough to help them in doing household chores. Guard tells me I am old enough to do my homework on my own. So, they are just being diplomatic towards me. I some time dislike the way Dad dresses, I like when he wears suit and tie. What the adjustments one has to make to get along.

Guard does small compromises with Grandma. They are getting along for the last 40-50 years. That is sensible. Now my Grandma is dieting with alternate vegetarian and non-vegetarian diet. She was carnivorous and now she tries to become herbivorous. It is good of public school education that I am able to learn such hard and sometimes difficult words. Well it is my business to learn grammar, composition, punctuations and synonyms and antonyms. When I am learning complicated words, I can hear complicated stories. No big deal. But math, I could never like. Why should we learn the tables, addition, subtraction, etc. when we have calculators to do all that and save time and energy?

I also don't know why Momma does not use words like 'honey', 'sweet heart', 'darling' and 'dear', as other mothers use for their children. Why my parents are not in habit of telling bed-side stories, like stories of fairies, princess, and other small stories of rabbit and tortoise, or fox and stark. I am not past the age of story-telling, my younger sister is not interested in stories. She tells her stories, which both Momma and Dad listens. Guard is only interested in telling stories about his friend GC. I believe he considers himself a genius, which is not true.

Once he was referring to GC, that because of his lean thin stature and starched long coat, he is mistaken as someone carrying a coat on a hanger, which is sufficient motivation for him to gain weight if his circumstances allow, which was a meagre hope among many. How is it possible? I always wonder. But Guard can manipulate his stories, he can impersonate characters, he can fabricate the themes and miscalculate the time zones.

He is getting pretty old and forgetful. He forgets names and numbers, but he can remember faces, old or new. He calls it photographic memory, as though he is a photographer, capturing images and storing them in his mind.

He would say, 'Mom, you are special because of your color'.

'What about whites'?

'No, they are not special'. What a racist he is.

'Oh! Don't call me that', he said. I could be put to prison based on your 2nd amendment'. But he is a free bird chirping whatever he likes.

'This is the advantage of 1st amendment', he said, 'Freedom of speech'.

His problem is, he takes a long time to load his pipe and light it and blow blue smoke in the air, letting others to wait. Once I asked him about the hazards of passive smoking. 'Don't worry, you are getting immunity and there is more smoke in the streets than in this room'. Was his explanation.

If I tell Grandma, she will read some supplication in Arabic and blow at me. She would tell me stories about her bridal dresses with matching jewelry, she would tell me tirelessly stories about her long stay in North Africa, which will not end and I found them boring. Dad will talk about his geriatric patients. My Aunt will talk about religious stories and my Uncle would tell the same old story of the mouse, which was roaming around and stuck a thorn in his tail, he went to a barber, who cut his tail by mistake. Since then that mouse was still roaming around without his tail. What a diverse group of people living under one roof but getting along with such diversity.

Prosperity in diversity was American dream and the success story. They talk big but remain desperate. They are unlucky guys, who boast about their good luck. Good luck or bad luck, when it can't be helped, why should one worry about it. I wouldn't worry about other's luck. Luck is a chance factor, Guard would describe it. Chances come and go and so is the luck, is my opinion about luck too. And why to bother about transient factors. I told him, that people say bad luck is always followed by good luck.

'But it would be followed by bad luck again, so stop worrying. For that matter, hard work can change luck', was his final word on 'luck'.

'And good partner is also a matter of luck', he wanted to continue but I left him. I was getting tired by his logic.

'I am getting headache'.

'Take aspirin'.

'No, they are tension headaches, given by you people'.

Guard watches TV news as though he is preparing for some exam. I hate TV news, more so election coverages. What difference who wins. They show footages so repeatedly that you feel like switching it off and watch next day to get updated with what is new. Then they will invent some drama and scandal about something which gets faded off in no time. Guard told me who hasn't affairs in the past.

Past should be forgotten and future prospects should be looked into. Everybody tells me to focus on my aspirations, what I would become, how I could be successful, how I can get good scores, ranks, marks and grades. I better become a writer. I have descriptive narration skills and I use monologues than dialogues. I use first person over third person.

It is not mere con-incidence that I am not a competitive type, as competitive types bring curiosity, but I am curious about many things. Curious about the existence of this world, Adam and Eve, their sign languages, their progeny, their punishment or trial, these civilizations, these races, these sects, this ecological balance for existence, these divisions of provinces, these differences in cultures, these traditions, these people and these families. This old man, Guard. I recollected the phrase about think of the devil and there he is. Guard called me to complete the pending home assignments from school, to be completed in time to rehearse for the vocal music lessons, which were fixed for the weekends.

He was fond of old melodies and Ghazals which have certain preludes, but he was not good at inter-ludes. He usually gets lost in lyrics but he would continue with his rhyme and rhythm with pitches and notes. He would break down with high notes so he used to prefer the intermediate notes. A hazard of smoking.

He has been smoking for the last 50 years and what a time span to survive this long time of smoking to get away with occasional episodes of bronchitis and he used to treat himself. He seemed tired today, as he closed his eyes and was thinking. It was an indication that he will chat at that given time. He had the first-generation old mobile phone and first-generation laptop and an old antique pen probably gifted or purchased from some pawn shop, all seem to be from the time of renaissance.

He had many friends of different faiths and he used to respect them. He was fond of attending their festivals when colors are thrown on each other, when gun-powder crackers were lit and when some idols were displayed at all corners of the streets to be immersed in water after a period of time. He used to get plenty of greeting cards and plenty of letters, which he would sort out in leisure times. I had high hopes about myself and I bet Guard would differ. He doesn't like betting.

He thinks betting is to satisfy selfish gratifications and to get the pleasure of beating others by winning. I think he is a masochist, who doesn't self-pity but tortures himself to remain on principles. He would burst out laughing then suddenly stops, and sobs like crying and regain his cycle of laughter. I think he does that to recreate me. What a God forsaken old pitiable person he has become.

Guard has a crazy habit of collecting gifts which do not come in use and would repack them and keep them hidden somewhere. He had once returned the same gift to the same person by mistake and that person's face was swollen with feelings. He would bring a topic under discussion and casually slip away to do what he had already planned for himself and then claim that it was done after joint consensus.

He somehow manages to get through hurdles and hardships, like speed breakers or cracks in the roads or high tides of sea waves. He liked communism and not capitalism, some words I have leant but may not define them myself. Whatever I would get good gifts on my birthdays and would wait for the next year with curious interest.

Talking about gifts reminded me yet another incident of Guard's friend GC whose son got an unexpected gift from a thief. It so happened that one day a thief entered GC's house in the night with obvious intention but was disappointed to find any valuables and duly frustrated found a half open trunk which he quickly applied latch and carried it with him. Later he found GC's son sleeping inside in side it and next day came back to return the kid. Thief told GC that it is shameful that next morning the child was crying because of hunger and thief had to serve him south-Asian breakfast.

GC was amazed at the sequence of events and told him, 'What about the other kids? What is their fault to get deprived of the same breakfast'? Then it was thief's turn to get amazed. I took some time to understand the humor behind the scene but liked it.

I am not dumb or retarded. Where is my class? Where are those familiar faces gone? What is this system of teaching discipline to students? Why one has to call if one is getting late or not coming to school? Do they think kids can cheat their parents, invent lies to avoid going to school? Why in the middle of the day the attendance register goes to office and they come to know someone has absented and then they call home to find out?

Whoever lifts the phone has to give some convincing reason. It is like a criminal investigation and one is asked to show the alibi. What a method of completing a formality for the sake of system and not for the sake of discipline. But I will accept this reality and accommodate the system.

There are neatly and correctly comprehended sentences with fixtures of grammar and punctuation spoken in my class. I have never heard this crap before. Sentences are used to speak one's mind to the other. I don't want images of schools with such descriptions which were never heard before. This is not a gift for me. I am supposed to choose phrases from my mind for my survival. It is like asking for a freshly barbequed steak and getting an oatmeal cereal.

The worst part is home assignments, given so much that by the time I complete it gets darker and I have to swallow a hurried meal to go to bed. I have to do the home assignments without fail, otherwise the same will have to be redone in the recess time as a punishment. What a funny part of school education that one gets repulsed with the work. The manufactured products of the school turn out into complete fools. Forced to study against their wish with no motivation and no encouragement.

Studying in somebody's view point is student dying. It is garbage of suffocated minds, who are going by the book and not going by the benefits. I am already disciplined and do not require any thing more or less. I don't want anybody to teach me more discipline than what is required for my age. Why can't even discipline be taught gradually, like spellings. What is hurry? Our experiences will teach us discipline sooner or later. I would prefer to be later.

It rarely happens but it happened. Rare things do happen. Once one brown colored monkey entered our house, in the east. It coolly walked up to the frig, opened the door, saw inside for some eatables. Most of them were packed in microwave containers and while he was taking a detailed inspection, Guard was sitting watching the 'National geographic' channel where monkeys were shown, about how they enter villages and steal the food. He mistook it as part of the seen.

All this I have heard later, as I was riding my tricycle in the portico. Grandma saw the scene from the kitchen and ran into her bedroom. Monkey got alarmed and decided to walk out, but not before he jumped and sat on my shoulder. We exchanged glances, his was that of fear and mine was that of fright. He casually walked out and the drama was ended in an anti-climax.

I liked Monkeys as Guard had shown their activities to me in the local Zoo. I liked their funny ways and their frantic chases and their grimaces and their smiles or anger to the onlookers. But I liked the section of birds more than the wild animals. How they used to chant and make noises and show their colorful wings and would never sit at one place for long.

They always seem restless and crying for liberation. Why should they be caged was their first slogan to me. Once I even attempted to open their cage door, but I was prevented by a watchman. I believe in olden days, pigeons used to deliver letters instead of postmen. What an interesting fact. I wished a pigeon brings me letters too. But it was my wishful thinking.

As I see people walking home from work, they are mostly engrossed in thinking about something and occasionally collide with other pedestrians. But they never seemed to be in a hurry, like in west. Where urgency had crept into them as part of life. They do everything in haste. I was told by Guard that things done in haste could go wrong warranting repetition, they must be facing the same results.

But I have to think of many things, while coming home from school. I wanted to stop at the vendors and buy a soda, but again elders object saying that carbonated drinks are harmful for children. They can cause acidity. I was not asking for hard drinks. Elders are fanatics. Seriously it is hard to cross 10th year and still kept prohibited for quite a few things.

Guard used to say 'Teens' are a borderline between childhood and adulthood. So many years in between. He said he had never faced 'Teens', he crossed them and went from childhood to adulthood in a leap. It was his choice. But probably he was referring to the hardships he had faced during his teens that he had hardly enjoyed the liberty and freedom and was kept involved in completion of responsibilities.

His father, I was given to understand died when he was toddler and lived a life of deprivations since then. I heard children studying under street lamps, but good thing he did not mention such horrific stories. He used to give private tuitions while he was himself studying.

The discussion was turning very serious, so he shifted the topic to his friend GC, when once his father-in-law crossed him in the hall. Unlike other old people he has bent backwards and had high stepping gait. GC watched him with interest and he was enquired about his curiosity.

He replied 'It looks as though his father-in-law is peddling a bicycle without a chain'.

I am sure his wife was accustomed to such cracks and had never seemed to mind. Even Guard used to remain serious as though he is narrating a pathetic story.

'Comedy or tragedy'? I enquired.

'Tragedy'. Was his reply, but I knew he just said it without meaning it and we used to laugh a lot. Guard was fond of awful stares, awful jokes, awful descriptions, awful laughter and awful pretentious sobs, every thing which he would do awful initially but had been a fun for me, as he used to act out in such a manner to entertain me.

There were times when I got angry at him and screamed my lungs out, the he would put his finger on his lips and make a gesture of 'Silence', as though he is a poster seen in hospital corridors of a nurse asking people to remain silent. People are weird, better still insane. They boast a lot and show pride.

Guard says pride and prejudice are like wood worms which destroy the habitat not like silk worm which at least makes a fine fabric. People do not let people to live and let live. People make imaginary relationships based on crooked hatred but would stretch their lips to smile to fool around with themselves. The fact will come out in the end. I would make history.

But actually, what do I want to become? I would not stand beside a xerox machine to let it print as many copies as it wants. I want to dictate the genuine ingenious work and would ask the steno typist to take it in short hand. It is better in my books to avoid wasting time in obeying orders. I am not going to do baby-sitting for some cry some infants.

It is like eastern washer women trying desperately to remove certain stains from worn out clothing. I really don't know how to know. I am an American and should behave like one. I should plan to go all those places advertised in the travel brochures to attract customers to spend money and go there and get lost. Everyone needs to struggle to survive but earn money with dignity.

My money is earned with dignity and I put coins in my piggy bank. I think I should stop doing that, instead should put hundred-dollar bills neatly folded to get rich. I should not waste money on toys or junk food. I should collect all models of smart phones as a hobby, which I can sell if required. Or let them become antiques with time. With the money I will form a trust to help the homeless. Why they don't do anything and just remain homeless. Or I should become a stylist or a designer and charge heavy fee from the rich.

'What do you think, Guard, why shouldn't I become all at one time'.

'You may try but do things according to your capacity'. Was the answer.

'You may do one more thing, don't take elevators', instead get into habit of climbing stairs'. He added.

'How if it is 120 floor Empire state building'? there was no answer.

I recollected the time when my Dad proposed Momma in the east, I was sure he thought the children would be middle eastern, Arabic speaking. What a strange family of strangers uniting with different talents and different capabilities. What a diverse role playing under a single roof. Guard wants salad, Grandma wants fried ground beef meat balls, Momma wants chicken soups or chicken drumsticks, Dad wants nothing, Uncle wants barbequed items, Aunt wants vegetarian food and I want little bit of everything but my sister wants only sweets. Our kitchen looks like a mess at times. That is enough. Rather more than enough.

In this world girls are crowned for their beauty and grace. I thought I should fight for girls, why they are less fortunate than what they are. Who think browns are not as beautiful as whites and hence cannot be crowned, just because of their color. I wanted the to tell their stories, even if they are for themselves. I wanted them to write about their experiences, experiences of their struggle and wars that they have fought for themselves in their young ages, about the spoils of war they have acquired. Even if they have faced defeat and defamation. Wars are wars.

If someone looks at my face, they might find something is wrong, but if they look at my smile, then there is nothing wrong. I have won an undeclared war with myself. I should think about myself only. I am not responsible for other's lives. It is out of my habit to even give any opinion about them. Moreover, I am not a social worker to think, consider and bear other people's problems. I had my own story to tell. I have no resources except my own experiences. People say experiences give wisdom, which helps people to achieve success. I have to move and adapt to new surroundings. Let's see.

I believe I have to pass an entrance test to qualify for the system's age-old rule. Children are sent to schools to learn, not to qualify themselves first to learn later. If they are not good enough, then what do they have to do. Burn their books, paste the ashes on their faces like natives and dance wildly. This is the time to prove myself. When I was young I had lesser capability, lesser responsibility and lesser choices. But now I have to be a model of the society. I cannot be a model until I change drastically. But I cannot grow beard and wear a tall Turkish cap with a bushy string hanging from the top to look different. I cannot become the president and talk whatever I wish. Mostly surprises. I cannot become cow-boy girl and wear a gun slinger and a hat and ride a horse, wearing tall leather boots.

I better become Malala, sponsored by the west to demean the east, who gives press releases made by script writers, maybe she only lip synch while some British is speaking on her behalf. I don't know what sort of family support she had. I have to please my family. Family is a liability to me. Let the family get into my shoes and feel how it may look to them from my perspective. I should better learn magic and conduct shows giving surprises to people.

Or be a joker in a circus who has to paint his face white and wear a rubber ball on his nose and do some somersaulting to make people laugh. Or I better be a puppeteer behind the scene and play the dolls with strings. My life has become a comedy. Like a cartoon movie of Tom and Jerry, Sarah and duck and Donald duck, etc. I have to watch these cartoons with my younger sister to please her and the family.

Well I can do all these things but later. Now is the time for thinking. Deep thinking in shallow waters or Benji diving in thin air or riding a motorcycle in a well, like in old times shown at the end of the circus. Or I should become an actor in a Godforsaken movie, playing a leading role of a lady, singing songs round the trees or become a heroine of a horror movie to appear and disappear on the screen in dark nights or I just yawn and yawn until I go to sleep.

But I don't even know whether I will remain in east or west. West is colder and east is warmer, not weather wise but affection wise. You get warmth of love and affection in the east and you get forced pretentious smiles and nothing else in the west. In the east people laugh and cry but in the west people hide their feelings.

In the east one could smell the natural fragrance of dry earth evaporating after the first monsoon shower, one could get the fragrance of cuisines while passing, vendors, restaurants or hotels, even huts. Fragrances including festivals, celebrations, of forests with eucalyptus tree leaves falling with breeze in the parks and public gardens.

In the west one can get smell of air fresheners, chewing gums breaths, candy full of mouths or you have to go to a bakery and stand beside pretending to read a new paper, full of discounts and 'free' offers, which is meant to cheat, as there is nothing which is free. In the east countries are full of populations. Large populations struggling to survive and are lagging behind almost going astray.

I better stay quite and stay put among relations with love, kindness, affection, support, prayers and worship, more so when I don't even know whether I am a 'desi' meaning local or 'pardesi' meaning immigrant. Desis are supposed to submit to their parents and 'pardesis' are supposed to revolt against their parents. In any case I made a friend in my new school. A good friend, who I intend to make my best friend. I heard Guard telling me once that friend in need is a friend in deed.

So, my friend told me that last summer was the worst for her. She started crying. She became silent and cried again. I believe she lost her puppy dog due to heat exhaustion and while narrating it she started crying again, the memories must be very sad for her.

I hugged her, her tears wetting my shoulders. I felt odd with my wet shoulders both for a change. I waited upon her to give me the details. Guard always tells me to listen to grieved friends. She couldn't continue. I think she had a similar as that of mine, but I could be wrong. I was having difficulty with my spoken English.

I was just being courteous and not curious, in spite of somebody telling me that as long as you have curiosity, desire, willingness and of course some disconcert, you will go ahead in life and become successful. People say different things at different times. I shouldn't be too much concerned about them. I should be curious with myself and avoid expressing it.

It looks like sarcasm, which is there in my blood. Guard is sarcastic, Grandma is sarcastic, closed and distant relatives are sarcastic, but not Momma or Dad. They are straight forward people. Momma could be humorous but not sarcastic. So, where from I got this sarcasm, I must have learnt from Guard only. A sarcastic person, who would not mind hurting other's feelings. He says it is necessary at times. At times?

Sarcasm could make some people laugh and some people cry. No wonder I could undertake sarcasm at the appropriate times. A balance in sarcasm is itself a sarcasm. At the same time when others get sarcastic, I should not be disappointed. What goes around, comes around. My Momma's favorite phrase. But why disappointments have been made a part of life. I can't lose anything which I didn't have.

I am not going to get standing ovation for it but I found standing ovations very gratifying. I had nothing better to do, except to vocalize my tone and verbalize hard words. But who cares for standing or sitting or stooping or lying down ovations. My Momma told me that Ohio river does not belong to Ohio, it is taken by Kentucky, all new names of new places I was getting acquainted with.

Mostly from Guard. I think he is wise enough to grow beard and retire for good. He becomes boring as he never is tired of teaching, a hazard of being a teacher himself for so long. I believe he teaches graduate doctors for their post-graduation. Good for him but not for me.

If he grew up in cold mid-west and feel snow settling on his beard, more so after several shifts of school before the age of 10 years, he would have a different idea about giving lectures at university or at home. He would find different tomato ketchups with different contents, very much alike. In another 10 years I will become a better performer than him. How does it matter if I had been a shifting student, not on exchange program?

But in another 10 years I will be a better performer than Guard, in singing, painting, writing and speaking. For a kid to become a performer is good. I only needed encouragement, not from Guard alone. Poor fellow he will encourage me for everything, even without concentrating on what he is encouraging.

I want to write my story, which should be interesting. I should end it in anti-climax. What is an anti-climax? I think it is bifurcation of story which ends at the fork. To let the reader, decide which way they want to carry it forward. Their likes are equally important. No. No? Yes. Co-incidentally bifurcated. Right. No. Diabolically bifurcated. Yes. This is more appropriate. No. Not exactly.

I better quit. I better get accommodated and adjusted with what I have in hand. I should be contented with 'Ice-fruit' of the east like 'Popsicle' of the west. Or I better get my wish tattooed over my forearm. I had to shift now even the school but across seven seas into a new system and asked to feel at home. Where is my home. I feel homeless now.

What is feasibility? Simple, it means getting accommodated with what is provided. Is it because I am accommodating? That is how my first day at the public school started here. I should be contented with what is provided. I need not be more curious about the system of education in public schools. That is the rule for the game of life, to live in harmony. What a sentence. I can create words and sentences.

I have creativity, sensitivity and reactivity. I have not come here for a reunion of some sort, to exchange 'Hallmark cards'. I am not here to nurture 'Barbie doll' cultural revolution. I am myself a piece of art, in its own right. I would accept anything. All these cultural shocks to be absorbed. Let them leave some impact, some permanent marks on me. The trouble with the words is they are just words. Guard does the same and I would do the same. Playing around with words. Do I miss him? No. why should I for that matter?

He himself told me that past is past. Past cannot be relived, so better forget about it. But I asked him whether he is accompanying me. He casually replied to go ahead and that he would join me later. It was some kind of consolation. As Momma usually tells 'You wait for a minute and I will join you in 10 minutes'. When he will join me then I will miss him, not until then. He is a crook and not worth remembering.

His favorite slogan which he used to utter so often that I almost byhearted. 'Don't break the expectations of parents'. But it all depends on the expectations and their kind. At some other time, he himself said that 'High expectancy levels are not good for normal living'. If you counter him, I know he will come up with some explanation and some justification.

What a junk food he was, which is not good for absorption or assimilation. He used to say, 'Don't go astray with junk food and with faith'. When I am sure he was also fond of junk food. Junk food for children and not for seniors. I wish I could have told him at his face, bluntly. Especially after having witnessed myself about his venturing junk food behind closed doors.

Talking about his expectations, he expected his children to be like him and his children expected him to be like them. What a parody of comparisons. What an irony of expectations. The same holds true with his tolerance thresholds. Such ideologies and such philosophies talking to a girl of my age. How does he expect me to understand? His words were like traps, lies, which are going to get drowned with him. All those artistic facts.

Art is art, fine art is truth, reality is faith and motivation is belief. What I know of art was different. Art should be pleasing to the eye. I can publish my art in the school journal. I have dome some masterpieces of art in my diary. I think I should writing my diary again.

Writing diary keeps me occupied and forget the unpleasant. Diaries keep surveillance of my activities, like video surveillance in a fashion boutique. Where costly garments are worn by mannequins against their wishes. Poor mannequins that they can't refuse or can't change even if they don't like them. Diaries can fix many issues. Important and un-important. Half lies or half-truths. They can escape complaints and grievances.

When I was born I was full of crap, but now I have grown up and can turn everything upside down. That is the way world should expect from me. More so after several shifts of residences, schools, communities and nations and continents. Now all would depend on me. As was rightly said 'People get what they deserve'.

My regret is to have been born in this world. I think I should have been better off on some other planet. Or as people say was I changed in the nursery by a wrong wrist or foot band of someone else. I feel I am a rose bud, about to blossom and emit fragrance and about to be picked for a bride's garland ring of roses to be worn but perished in the process by harsh weather. As though I have to be proclaimed star but became a janitor.

I am not in deep trouble to just smile and pretend nothing has gone wrong. Life in this world is pain in excess. I will try to modify it and shape it better for others.

I can become a highly paid model for just cat walking on a ramp. I can cat roll for good payment. It is advantage to remain a kid. You can throw punch lines or even real punches and could get away. What a privilege to enjoy? No, not really. I was just kidding. But one thing I am sure of is it is time for people to appreciate my efforts.

I am going through a rough hearing, rough trial and rough adjustment for adaptation to different experiences. It is not a minor accommodation. I am a major player in my history, my life history. I can't be taken lightly or neglected lightly. I don't ask for favors lightly which could be rejected lightly.

I can become a baseball player who could shoot a ball thrown at me crookedly turning it towards the empire, who would be hit and fall to the ground. I can stand menacing curved balls too. I am an unsung hero who write morbid letters but do not post them. I can leave impressions on people. I am an iconic figure who could do wonders, other than the already existing seven wonders of the world.

I can develop themes and imagine about angels and fairies. But I have to give up when I will cross teens. Guard went into depression when President Kennedy was assassinated and I was amazed at his attachment to that handsome man. I will brood now on martin Luther King's assassination. He was a great man greater than Mohamed Ali Clay, Malcolm X or Michael Jackson.

But I wish ISIS is assassinated. But organizations cannot be assassinated. In any case why should I bother about mad people, insanely sane or sanely insane. Guard narrated the story of his friend GC, when he confessed that he was assassinated.

'Oh! Come on how can an assassinated person talk about himself', I couldn't help interrupting.

'No, he meant, caught as though assassinated when his friend's lender found him with over due debt and he climbed the tree'.

'Climbed the tree'. I interrupted him again.

'Yes, not even that his friend called him from up and asked him to follow up'.

I was stunned imagining the drama associated with the scene.

'Did the lender followed him', I again was helpless to believe.

'No, he was a fat man, unlike GC'. I had to believe him. Guard's friends could do such things.

I had 100% tolerance to stupidity and Guard had 0% tolerance to stupidity. He wouldn't mind singing and playing instrumental music to entertain buffaloes. I have learned other skills to show off. I don't switch off vacuum cleaners for the fear that they may not start again. Unlike smart phones which can be switched on and off any number of times.

I can become a movie star as I have to nod my head to make believe Guard that I am listening, even if I am just acting out. I can do flattery with myself to please me. But I don't like to flatter others. They will become proud and will start boasting high of themselves. Pride is disliked by God, I was told many times by elders, by elders I mean Guard, who else. He has a listening ear and he will talk.

'You know something or I told you before', I was in a mood of boasting.

Guard was all ears to me. I was in a running race competition and at the shot of the gun, toy gun of course, I ran and ran and ran and stopped only to collect my prize. Out of habit may be and I will keep running in or out of competition. I immediately repented as it gave an excuse to Guard to narrate another incident of his friend GC.

I believe GC's son was eating an ice-cream cone and when he saw his maternal Grandfather he ran, but he was chased and caught by the old man, who ate the rest of the ice-cream.

Once I believe, in his father-in-law's presence the boy narrated this story in GC's ear and he looked at him in amazement.

'Get lost. You should not tell these things in public'. Was GC's curt reply to his son, who escaped humiliated.

His wife enquired, as to why the boy was given this tongue lashing and he narrated the entire story with unwanted additional attention to detail. His wife was unexpectedly did not mind the espionage, as probably she is aware of her father's weakness for ice-creams.

At another time his father-in-law appeared suddenly at the door. GC enquired about his welfare.

He answered, 'No, I was passing by and felt like seeing my daughter as whenever I see her, my hunger is satisfied'.

GC looked grimly first at the old man and then at his daughter and said, 'is she your daughter or fried mutton'.

'Don't tell me'. I uttered speaking to no one.

'Okay, I will not tell you'. He replied. Oh! My lord, it was a phrase, used locally. I told him the same.

'Is it a comedy or tragedy'?

'Comedy, of course and for your kind information, Mom. I use it more often than not. He laughed and I didn't. I found it a sarcasm.

I had to find out, 'Is it a sarcasm or humor'.

'Sarcasm of course'. Then we both laughed and laughed. This is the way his friend's short stories kept coming in between and we used to enjoy, some times genuinely and sometimes pretentiously.

On the contrary my Dad hardly cracks a joke and my Momma always cracks jokes. Like father, like daughter, I have heard somewhere. Especially on phone she could talk and talk, as I could run and run. Very unlike mother and daughter. No competition, no prizes and we continue in our routines. She does her job and I do mine.

This is typical of eastern culture and I belonged to west. I have sandwiched myself between east and west. My Momma was more concerned about my lean and thin stature and wanted to feed me more, but my younger sister had a bigger mouth and she would wipe out the plates in no time. It won't matter if Dad has to work all day seeing his patients and Momma has to spent all day with her customers. Nothing mattered to both of us except junk food.

Once I believe, Guard's friend GC's kids came fighting and complained that the younger one was eating bricks and sand. GC listened or not, but casually spoke to both.

'No, no. you must not fight. Just share and eat'.

'But, Guard how can a father tell his children to eat sand'? I could never understand this logic.

'It is a joke'. Guard was serious.

'How'? I insisted.

'Comedy, Mom comedy'. And we laughed. Guard should try acting in a cow-boy movie. Galloping on horses, making faces and cracking jokes and laughing comically. How if he has a beard to wear and he would look like a religious cow-boy. I found a chance to corner him. Now my face was showing made up anger and I scolded him.

'Why don't you pray like Grandma'. He looked at me, pretended fear and said with his gaze at the floor.

'Mom, I pray in solitude'.

'Solitude'?

'I mean when I am all alone'. He has justified here as well.

He was different and I am different. I like when people see me praying. But I don't like to be a scout or guide. I don't want to visit old age homes and sing songs for them, who appear disinterested in my songs, but of course nod their heads with pasted smiles. They want the social service after the entertainment.

I am interested in comics, cartoons and would want to check on Santa if he has not missed my gifts like last Christmas. Am I being selfish? Guard himself says, that some bit of selfishness and some bit of anxiety is good for health. His logic and his reasoning. To hell with it. To hell with him.

I have to develop my own reservations. Is it a correct usage of the word? I mean, I cannot be a hostage in a bank robbery to be used for negotiations between robbers and police. Why can't robbers trick a policeman and make him a hostage. This is clear violations of human rights. What are human rights?

They are not life lines attached to terminally ill patients to prolong their suffering. Quality of life is important than the quantity. All this is good for nothing. Rather I would prefer robbers than police. Poor people they don't have money and so they rob. Human rights do not allow ISIS to be brought to courts. They neither did with Nazi fascists. Governments are formed by politicians. Politicians are nuts. Government officials are careless fools. They just follow the routine to keep getting their salaries.

Once a government health inspector, visits Guard's friend GC's house. And gave a rehearsed speech for 10 minutes about the Malaria eradication program and governments efforts to control it, all in one breath. GC listened patiently and asked, 'Have you finished'?

'Yes. Why what is wrong'?

GC announced, you have forgotten one thing'.

'What was that'? he questioned.

'Thanking you, yours faithfully'. What did he mean by that I questioned Guard.

He answered, 'It completes the application, which he has so well-rehearsed'. I took time to absorb it but when I did, I kept laughing and laughing.

I am getting freaked out as it feels like a strange place. I looks like a desert with wide spaces and I am beginning to hate it. Some people end up here, declared unlucky, at least in my case, I am sure about it. It was not a good idea to have been born in this place. The secret thing is your parents should not have come here at all. Gambling on American dream.

I am a good girl basically, but I might become one like them with passage of time. I was intended to be tossed out but fate interfered and I was obliged to return. Again, parent's fault and not mine. When I am practically here I am a lonely face in the vastness. No body would know me, whether I go out or remain in. I am writing and may continue doing so, but it does not guarantee me any company.

I would become a different person, in search of happiness or contentment as Guard often uses this word. I think both are the same. If I am not happy how could I be contented. My Dad will be here, my Momma will be here, my younger and elder sisters will be here, all elders with acquainted faces will be here, my new-found friends will be here. My Dad has money, my Momma is making money and more than that they have respect. Money and respect are both relative things, Guard used to say.

More than money and respect, life is important, more than profession and more than career. There can be two persons in the same profession one successful and the other not in their careers. There can be two successfully placed persons in a career, one happy and the other unhappy in life. So, life is important in the end.

When I first came here I felt I already knew the place, like a flamingo know the fish in shallow waters or a circus lion know when to roar in his den. All my imagination created out of color pictures turned out to be fake. My Momma says this place is for 'have nots', retards and morons who aim to get lucky but they never draw a lottery ticket. People come and go.

There is continuous rotation, but not revolution. Rotation is like winding on a top and revolution is like making progress, immaterial of weather changes. I was comfortable in my old house, everything was good except door-bell which used to become annoying at times. I was any other girl with admixture of color shades. I never felt out of place.

I didn't like music as music was inside my head playing different instruments all times. I liked folk music, as it makes you move in the beginning and dance in the end. I heard about a man who jumped out of his balcony and cracked all his bones and upon asking as to why he did it. He said just like that. I think he was imagining bungy jumping. He lived by and lived by. But it was not a good idea to get engrossed in imaginations to the extent that, one loses touch with reality.

This appeared to be a place where people shake hands for the sake of shaking hands and may even ask questions of welfare without meaning them. Fake hand-shakes, fake people, fake society, fake diversity and fake prosperity. As such I was tired of life, not that we were below poverty lines, but everyone was concerned about savings and making their savings to come handy in times of rain. I believe it is also a phrase, as in the east there is a full 4 months season of monsoon and in the west, there will be unexpected rains at unexpected times and places. People have to carry backpacks with built in umbrellas.

So, why to save for rainy days? Here cash means nothing but luck means everything, cash comes and goes but luck remains. Now that I am here in the west, I have to get used to everything which everything which goes around and comes around. I needed my family but they needed me more. But this is weird place to live permanently. Temporary visits are good. Here rents are exorbitant and land lord don't come to collect them. It is all through a system of deductions.

This reminded me of Guard and his narration of his friend GC whose land lord comes to collect the overdue rent and GC's wife complains to him that the land lord is reminded to erect the back wall, because she said, 'Yesterday late evening one donkey entered the premises'.

GC was shocked to hear it and asked the land lord directly. 'Have you visited us last evening'. Then I didn't catch the humor or sarcasm, but now I understood it, that GC was referring his land lord to a donkey, in spite of his over due rent. How witty to live a life like GC?

When I was carried to the multi storied building and saw the scenic beauty of down town sky scrapers, I was impressed for few minutes then it was a routine view, but I was also astonished that they are also poor people and didn't have ceiling fans, then I was told they have A/C boxes beside wall on the floor for heating and cooling. I was impressed again.

I was impressed by the antique furniture which didn't look any different that others. People were serious probably planning to welcome me. In the lobby there were sentry Guards saluting every visitor and they saluted me and I saluted back. They were surprised but kept cool. They could have misunderstood it as mockery. But they were blacks, so nothing made any difference.

When I went down I heard music loud and clear in my ears almost shattering my ear drums. To add to my suffering the solo drivers were trying to sing equally aloud. Probably deprived of entertainment and causing noise pollution. So, I have to hold on. I returned back and touched the sofas, table tops of thick glass, some tall uncomfortable chairs and big size TV, as you see in drive in movies. Among all these curio pieces I was feeling lonelier.

I do remember my past. East and fun which I had. My Dad was away and my Momma was away. My younger sister was not born yet. My Momma was a legend and I was an after-thought. I had developed a knack of living, my own style, my own paradise. I prayed Guard should be allowed to smoke his pipe in paradise. I hope smoking is allowed in heaven, or else he would apply to be transferred to hell.

Soon I was carried to a charity dinner meant for fund raising. Fund raisers in a prosperous country is a comedy in itself. Like non-profit organizations. Why do they function if there are no profits involved? Yet another comedy. Guard's memories came more often than required. Why did he insist me to go to west? To this uncanny world. But I didn't complain. I didn't want to let him down. At least I could make Momma happy and worry less about me in the east. Here gun culture also is rampant, my Dad told me. Why should I worry, I can also carry a gun in my shirt pocket protruding its nose to calm down the mobsters?

Once Guard told me that his father had a range of guns, short some long, some single barrel and some double barrel. I wish I should have asked me hand over all those guns and I would be feared here. I need not fear gun culture. 'Guns bring both good luck and bad luck, Guard said once. How it be possible a single item bringing both type of lucks. Guard is insane.

He also told me that his father married twice. So, what. It is not a big deal. Some

African clans have 20 or more wives. He also told me that his father did some heroic deeds and was awarded gold medals, which generated monthly pension to his two mothers all their life time. Guard casually told me that his father had 2 Dobermans as security dogs and 2 servants used to take care of them. I will have 2 pet cats.

Later I will have a bungalow like my great Grandfather, an imported Oldsmobile car, a chauffeur a butler and fleet of servants. I better not marry 2 husbands. Both will become pain in the neck. Or if both start abusing me, then I will have to go to Mohamed Ali Clay and taking boxing sessions. It would be waste of time. Like a waste land. Roses gardens should be the definition of wasteland. But nothing should matter to me.

I have important projects to complete. Even if I am losing on something, I should be completing my projects. Husbands are savages, Dad is an exemption. They are not worth a damn. Some wear hats, some Turkish caps, some wear straw hats and some wear peak caps. Where am I? why should I be discussing about them. No comparisons, no sacrifice, no justice, no pre-fixes, no post-fixes, no nothing.

I sometime think awesome but sometimes awful. I am a butterfly flipping my wings over roses. I care about people the way I do it doesn't make them feel it. I do other good things which I don't want to talk. I don't want to be a student carrying donkey load of books. Half-bent sideways to keep balance. Walk barefoot in snow, get drowned in books, get bored with teachers, get home to avoid homework, which I have to do if I like it or not. I have to evacuate in the evenings and sleep like a donkey, but not before I eat oatmeal cereal in the night. What a schedule for a day.

I went to London some time and I liked the place. The houses were intimately close, even if neighbors do not know each other for decades of living close by. The houses were neat, people were neat, but their smiles were fake. The only person with genuine smiles was my elder sister. She was understanding and cooperative. We had good time together.

Initially when I came here, I was put to play school. They calculated my age and declared fit for play school. It was fun. The school was nearby and we used to walk in summers within a ribbon ring distance across our house and we had plenty of play time.

Teachers were extra loving, which they are not supposed to be. Excess of anything is not good for health, was another oft repeated phrase from Guard.

Guard is never Guarded with his speeches. I think he has narcissi tendencies and likes to hear his own words resounding in his ears. He is attention seeker, like the boy who was described by Guard himself that once he fell down from stairs, when his mother was not around and reposted the incident on her arrival showing his abrasions and contusions.

His mother showed sympathy and enquired, 'You must have cried a lot'?

'No', was his reply, 'because you were not around'. Guard stopped abruptly again.

'So, what'? I had to ask him again.

'I don't know'. He made a cry-some face and the I started laughing and he continued crying. I knew he was pretending.

He stopped abruptly as usual and told me, 'Mom', you know once GC's son went back to GC's wife crying loudly. He was taking hiccups and making funny sounds but was genuinely crying. His mother had to show mercy on the poor boy and enquired the reason. He took time is describing while continuing crying and what was understood by his mother was that GC was hammering a nail in the cement pillar and he hit his thumb.

'Oh! Come on dear, this is a small mishap and on such petty incidents, you should not cry, rather you should laugh'. his mother advised.

'Yes, I did the same'. The boy cried out aloud. This time Guard laughed to start with and his laugh was infective and I laughed too. Then I understood that the crying was because he received a slap on his face from GC himself, for having been laughed at.

Slowly I started liking this place. Slowly started liking Dad, slowly started liking Momma, slowly started liking snow fall, especially when I would be allowed to play throwing snow balls at others.

I couldn't make snow man, which I very wished. I wanted to place marbles in the place of eyes, let him wear an old hat and of course red colored pointed folded paper nose. I wanted to put a curved sea shell as for his lips and throw a scarf around his neck. Someday I will. Someday I will show it to my younger sister. She would love it. She always enjoys snow fall but not snow storms.

Once in winters she had slipped and hurt her butt. She wanted to cry, but she stopped when she heard my spontaneous laugh. but summers of this place were fun, not just because of long vacations, but also because we would swim in the swimming pool, splash water everywhere, feel hungry, get tired, eat hot dogs and sleep, with no wakeup alarms.

It would be green all around, flowers blooming and days will be longer and zoo timings extended for us to tease monkeys and feed ducks and sprout our tongues at the giraffe. We would go to lake shore and camp their till late evenings, watching the waves rising and foaming. We were allowed single piece swim suits but still I used to feel shy wearing it.

I missed Grandma, because she would have enjoyed more than kids. She would behave like a kid in company of kids, a teenager among teenagers, an adult with adults and an old woman still longing for youngsters to laugh, joke and play. She loved down town, lake shore, ladies garment shops and fancy restaurants to taste fancy food. One thing she would hate is museums and art galleries, in spite of her husband's likes. She was an absolute contrast.

She would complain about her increasing width but would never complain about her increasing age. Her passport was the proof of her age but she would say her father had increased her age intentionally. There was hardly a day when she would not be wearing a new dress. How manages to look new every day was a magic se alone would know and she will never share her secret with others. She would smile widely showing her dimpled cheek on receiving compliments and never get tired in attending to functions, all inclusive of marriages, birthday parties, graduation ceremonies and even funerals.

Her genes have made her children to develop a liking for branded clothing and designer wears. If she could help she may not hesitate to cat walk on ramps and shoot videos if not selfies for her craze to portray her pictures. She would always be running short of money because of her fondness for new clothes and she would be grieved if asked to window shop at the end of the month, when her pocket money gets exhausted.

Good thing she did not insist on credit card or got into habit of taking loans, which was not impossible for her. Jasmine flower garlands were yet another of her weakness. Probably it reminds her of her marriage. While Guard was allergic to jasmine and would get bouts of cough. I still do not know whether he genuine had it or pretend to avoid the liability of getting her garlands every day.

After parents get their children at hand, their purpose of life should change. They should be committed to serve them, raise them properly to make them responsible citizens. Guard used to say, parents get washed up in love for their children that they overlook the norms of up-bringing. Guard also used to say, if you are defeated unreasonably don't go for revenge, go for justice, as though justice is readily available on a plate garnished with righteous verdicts. Is he a moron or what?

I invited myself to be here, where I can be my original self. Relaxed, calm, composed and interested in life. A nickel, a dime or a dollar. All is well with me. Not doing anything. No parody, no mimicry, no mime or whatever. I wasn't a princess but I can be a saint. A messiah for my own self. A promise of paradise, promise given in a framed certificate. I have a story to tell to the America.

I am Miss. Perfect from the very beginning, from old times, even if they were not stone ages. Celebrating my destiny. Everything. I want to be myself, if not for wisdom at least for my story. I don't have the vague idea where I would have landed, where I would have been wandering and wondering what I should be doing. I have done certain compromises, which are unknown to elders.

I am going to miss myself. Now that I taught me how to live in the strangest places. This is wisdom for wise. I have lived right. I shouldn't bother what others would talk about me. I even don't know what this western society has to offer me. I have God with me. A just God, but there is no parable for God to be just or unjust. What is important is God had always been caring, kind and considerate to me. Loving and forgiving too.

That is what Momma always used to say. It is people who are unjust, thankless and deranged. What I know is, I should be doing justice with myself first and then to the world. The saying in the east is, first light your own lamp in the house and then carry an extra one to the mosque. I should be satisfied with myself.

I was given free will, Guard used to say. I could get up at any time I want, eat whatever I like and play for as long as I want. I am talking about school vacations. So, I was given free will during vacations, but school days were governed by fixed routine. I wonder why they cannot reverse the vacations and school days or ask the children to compensate for long vacation when they grow. Vacations are gift for kids, so they should be allowed to enjoy as much as they want.

In these worries, I forgot one incident which Guard had narrated about his friend GC. Yes, these are worries for me to get up with alarm clock, wriggle in bed till alarm stops, then I should be ready till the second alarm begins and then go to school and return home to complete the homework. At least home work should be completed in school hours only and the evening should be allocated for family time.

Yes, I recollected one incident which Guard had narrated about his friend. I believe on first of some month GC brought some cosmetics for his wife, which was an unusual gesture of sympathy more than affection. His wife enquired about the gift package and she opened it to find powder, foundation and lipstick.

'What for all this at this age'?

'No, my dear when house gets old, it needs fresh paint for renewal and renovation'.

GC thought his wife would be happy to receive it. She left it as it is and went to kitchen to get along with the household chores.

'Guard, that is unfair'. I commented and he ignored it, like GC's wife. When Guard happens to be in good mood, he will not restrict himself with a single incident.

He continued, 'And you know something', he was thinking whether he should continue or not.

'Once, there was sudden unexpected load shedding in the early hours of night and GC's wife said, 'Oh! Man, you have not shaved for few days'. She stopped, Guard stopped and I stopped. I failed to grasp the incident.

'What do you mean, can his wife see in darkness'? I asked. Guard was silent but I was putting pressure on him.

'How can it be possible'? I continued 'She is not a cat to see in black and white'.

'Maybe'. Guard was reluctant to go any further. I also forgot it completely and only now I recollected, but I still cannot explain as to how that lady could see in the darkness.

I had to get back to the realities of my adjustments. I was not unlucky. I should be grateful for my gifts of new clothes, new shoes, new belt, new hair brush, new socks and new head bands. I preferred double poly tails but Momma allowed only one and that too, high up to let it swing sideways when I would run or jog. I had to jog to survive here, I was told. Everybody jogs here, even if it rains o snows or sunlight. The routine was to jog. I had to be fit to survive not jog.

I should not lean upon others and I should be independent here. We don't get servant maids as in the east. Who are always around and happy to serve at any time. I can be dependent on God who is independent. I cannot be dependent on people who are in turn dependent on God. I should have a direct contact with God.

People should listen to me and listen to my story. Untold still. There has to be an audience, I cannot speak to an empty hall and empty chairs. I am not on a golf course, or a racing track or a running train. I am stationary at one point. I am where I should be. I am not a crude stone or an uncut diamond. I am a gem or a pearl not found yet.

I want to talk about who I was, who I am and who I will be. It is right in front of me. I have moved up a little and gone down a little. It is not my fault, it is the way people judge me. I did not do any big mistakes or blunders. I didn't have real hardships, just some road blocks, some cracked ditches and some speed breakers. I only have to jump but need not leap.

I have to look for a new life, new school, new friends, new backpack, new books, everything new, charming, glistening and glimmering. I should dream big and do small talk. I should be a genius but remain humble. All great people were humble. The open door in front of me takes me nowhere. It goes back to where I don't want to be.

I am not a clerk is a county hospital who only shift files from tables. I am my own door, I have to go through it to find me, my original self. There is a process and I will undergo it. I am fun and I am good. Between me and my reflection I am a jewel, spreading light rays to guide me. Better still is I being a jewel thief. A crime reporter, a cinematographer and a publisher to reject my own story to go unpublished. To publishers, young talented writers may go to hell.

No, I better be an astronaut to go to Mars and left stranded their all by myself. I would return like an alien, an alien like an undocumented, I will belong to another planet and would wander in another galaxy. I am an iconic person, with my life in Achilles tendon. I can't take it anymore. I would be laughing and talking to me.

My stares make people think they are monkeys and they start scratching their heads. I can orchestrate an opera or a melody which would become viral and I would become famous overnight. Then I would be wagging my tail on my own music. I am not being sarcastic here instead I am polite. I will not open up. I will remain shut. My story will be told by others.

Oh! People, I thought you are on my side. It is hideous. It is a footage worth kidding.

You have changed. I am not an idiot. Wars are lost because of lack of planning. What do they call 'strategic planning'? I want you to look at your miserable lives, how hard your lives were during colonial times, during civil wars, during times of oppression. It is only lately that 2nd amendment was introduced against the wish and will of racists.

They did not realize the uprising was mandatory and for legitimate reasons. Now this is the era of cold war. Now how many people are dying for any good causes. On the questions of clues, nobody knows. My statement is self-explanatory. I should go out for a breath of fresh air, as though I will get suffocated otherwise.

Let's do some math. Say out of hundred how many parents humiliate their children and abuse them. How many complainers, dirty politicians exist at a given time or how many are available now. Hoe many of you will be happy if your friends have gone away for good. Vanished from the world respectfully. Now how many of your extended relatives are maltreating others, you cannot count.

They are disordered people, mentally imbalanced, and how many of you would be happy if they are gone. I want them to be wiped away from the world. Just at the snap of my fingers they would disappear. Those who go to wars are cool, in spite of their families being unkind and un-loving. To conclude victims of wars are cool people. Good people, but they are not rewarded. Their names do not appear in the list of heroes. They are not rewarded for their gallantries.

I feel there is no shame is seeking help. Help is a need which all of us need. You would never know, who could be helpful or helpless for you in times of need. Help is a weapon like sleep is a weapon. Sleep can be collected by yourself after prolonged sleeplessness, or you can get sleep by sleeping pills, but help has to be sought from outside. So, help if it is made available.

Or else you have to remain engaged in civil wars forever. Civil wars changed the history of America. The biggest civil war was the most-unkindest cut of all. I read somewhere it was June or July the 1st that horns of success were blown. I think it in Gettysburg. Rebels arrived and burned the flags and the government retreated and thousands of soldiers died. So, what? millions died in Vietnam. Give me a break. I need not shed tears for any.

Our family was in wreck and became shattered in broken pieces. My mother fled, father escaped and I was looking out for a shelter for my caretakers. God was kind. I was provided with the requirements. There was a head of the family to run the show. The show went on and we survived. It was God's grace.

I was all wounded deep down, I cannot forget the sequence of events. I can't even forgive the reasons. Forgiving is close to forgetting. I couldn't do both. I am not being disrespectful, I have to talk straight. Talk is a parody of reality. I need to know the reality. People should listen, listen for the sake of listening. I know they can't do anything. They can't help others and for that matter they can't help themselves.

I have to seek the solution of my problems, it does not matter how. All have to listen and listen with undivided attention, with absolute sincerity, honest intentions and all must help me seek my solution. I have come to selfish society and my family has to be selfish with their consistence for sustenance. I get ideas but find them not very satisfactory.

I want some space to gather new ideas, one of which may suit my needs. It makes perfect sense of what I am doing. People are trying to present as everything is normal. Normal without normalcy. A break down from normalcy which I experienced as though I have fallen from a height deep down into trench. Normalcy has no criteria of norms. My normalcy may not suit others and other's may not suit me.

Everybody is different and especially here diverse, but clarity is required for harmonious living. Once I had a different kind of debate with Guard.

'Whose idea is this'?

'Does it matter'?

'Yes, it does to me'.

'You should say sorry'.

'Sorry'.

'No, it does not mean verbalizing only, one must feel sorry'.

'I feel sorry'.

'Good, the essential point for normalcy is keeping health, wealth, values and virtues'.

'Look at you, who is speaking'.

'It is you not me'.

'I knew I would be blamed in the end'.

'Don't blame others for who you are'.

'Yes, I am blaming myself for who I can be'.

Then we had a desert course, our favorite melting chocolate, with fruits, grizzled nuts, edible flower flavored with caramel salt and of course our banana foster with coco scent.

'You go ahead, I may not eat it'. Guard resigns when he loses a debate.

'Okay, what else I can get for you'?

'Just do me a favor and get lost'.

I started speaking to myself. I can understand, but it is never necessary that I agree and accept. There is no need to criticize and jump to conclusions. I can't help the inborn instincts and the traits. They may have genetic influence. I don't see a life like that. It is way out of proportion. Too outrageous. It was an accident, maybe an unfortunate series of accidents, but maybe coincidental. I am not coming back on stage to give a speech, rehearsed or not.

Decisions were not made by me. Decisions are a responsibility of elders. It starts ages before and may continue for ages to come. I cannot be held responsible. I should try to inspire mothers, abused mothers, single mothers, childless mother or mothers with many children, that they must face the reality and get over with heir hardships by will and determination.

I can't let people take a stand when I am tripping. It can't be a good idea to be a noble politician. Nobility and politics cannot go hand in hand. Prospects are getting reviewed they are being replaced by chance factors. Factors, conditions. Circumstances, etc., etc. This is what Guard always used to mutter, mostly to himself, but so often that I almost memorized it.

To me it is as though he is giving donation to a nameless organization and the accumulated funds are used by an offshore account for drug trafficking. Awful and unthinkable, but Guard is a man who does lot of pseudo-philosophical thinking and may not hesitate to execute his thoughts. Absurd. I myself had many problems, I cannot add others to it. Someday I hate it and someday I face it.

Everybody deserves a second chance. That is exactly is the need of the time. Then we can leave it to the fate, destined fate which God has written for us. But we have to make efforts from our sides first and then wait for the results. That is the deal God had offered. I am a deal maker and deal breaker, but I will stick to it and remain sticker for the reminder of it. I am a human being like others. Every point of view deserves child's approval but every child doesn't deserve all point of views.

There must be exemptions to rules. I can go to war for my family as an act of love for them. Becoming a war veteran is a fast or slow achievement. I am not sure of it. I have to redefine the color, odor and taste of the suffering and grief of separation which a family faces and the drama with surmountable amount of growth a nation is benefitted by.

I get dumb-founded by the knowledge of the fact that all circles down to money. Money and nothing else. I think everyone is mostly good, according to their over valued ideas. Important is one should have the sense of logic and reasoning and a sense of decency towards one another, this is yet another remark often repeated by Guard.

I vividly remember, which actually I don't want to, but it keeps coming back to me. There are certain things which cannot be helped. Guard's usual defensive comment on getting helpless. He was a helpless man, a worthless person and a hopeless creature to be true. Well I remembered flying on a 747 plane from east to west. The accompanied baggage was my Momma and my Aunt, the same surrogate mother in Momma's absence.

What a time of the day or small hours of the morning when we flew and the time difference due to time zone difference we landed in the day time or early morning. Planes land every where in the mornings to let the landers see the day light, as though they are brought out from solitary confinements of night's darkness. Who cares, what is the policy of airlines? At least I don't care, rather I don't want to care.

Oh! Sorry. I forgot to mention, that I also remembered Guard even before landing. Poor man, must be preoccupied in himself and maybe recollecting his friend GC. I sometimes used to wonder why he is preoccupied by his so-called friend, GC.

What a name he has coined for his friend 'Ginger Claws'. Ginger is ginger and claws are claws, but what a combination. I believe his friend was being nagged by his wife to send his pet cat, who used to swallow the leftover milk by stealing, from wherever she finds it.

A milk lover unlike me, who had refused milk from the beginning and we could have got along very well. Contrasts to survive the life to live. One being a milk lover and the other a milk hater. I wish milk should have had a shade of orange or pink or I wouldn't mind even violet. Even light brown would have done the purpose.

Anyway, so it so happened that GC's wife was tired of the cat and had been nagging on her husband to leave cat at some place from where, she gets lost. Get lost forever. Yielding to her wishes or her nagging, he took the cat to the next colony and left her and came back. He was about to take a sigh of relief that he found the cat in the door step. He was amazed. But cats find their way home.

Next day he took her to some far away residential colony and returned back and slept, as though he has sold his horses to sleep in peace. Next morning, he heard the cat's 'Meeaaoo' and resigned. His wife called him names which made him to shiver. Cats find their way back home. Next day he took the cat blind folded and took many circuitous turns and twists and turns and lost his own way back home by himself, to remove the blind fold and followed cat to reach home. He must have another sigh of relief.

This was a story in itself. And a tragic one this time. I was not to decide about it being tragical or comical. I think he used to make these stories, as such stories do not seem real. They can't be real for the simple reason that cat's photographic memory is put to challenge and she comes out a winner and her master turns out a loser. Guard was good at making stories. He should be a story teller, if not a fortune teller.

Talking about fortune telling, I believe Guard once went to a palmist and showed his palm lines to hear some good future forecasts. The palmist looked gravely at his lines and bylines and told him that half of his life will be spent in hardships. Guard became excited to hear about the other half.

'Then what?' was his suppressed excitement.

'Then nothing'.

'How come, nothing about the other half', he persisted.

'You will get used to it', was palmist's forecast. I am sure Guard have felt like crying but resisted the urge.

Among the hardships of Guard's life were the cats which used to make loud noises behind the bed room and used to wake him up. He would always be grumpy upon being awakened that way. One stray cat was a regular visitor and an ugly one I believe. Like the ugly 'Tom' unlike the cute mouse 'jerry'. I used to watch a lot of Tom and Jerry cartoons back in the east. Guard used to shove the cat by a loud 'Shyss'.

But one day Guard was annoyed to the extent that he found a cricket bat and swayed it in the air, like he wanted a sixer but which hit or didn't, but the ugly cat fell off the wall. Grandma was watching the scene. It was like a cat and mouse play, but in reversed order, with cat being the Guard and mouse being the cat. What an interesting cartoon it would have turned out. People would be telling stories of Guard and cat chase.

One could hardly predict Grandma's moods. She would be cheerful and doubtful or freaking or shrieking. She liked dresses and her daughters too, she would want parties and so would her daughters, she loved spicy cuisines and likewise her daughters, she loved pet cats and her daughters too but Guard preferred studies and his son not, he would like isolation and his son want company, he was a self-made man and his son was cultivated and he liked old melodies and his son liked pop music.

Guard would watch sports channels and his son would prefer cartoon movies. If I am given the option to vouch for one, I would go in favor of his son. This can't be the so-called generation gap. Gaps at some place and no gaps at other places. Our family was strange, if not weird and still had some common aims and objectives striving for common goals. I kept wondering and ultimately decided to let them do whatever instead of going to hell. As for me, I wanted heaven and all the goody goodies of heaven, without trying to earn them.

So, we landed in this vast country on the brightest day under the sun. it was late spring and the scenario of greenery and flowers in the gardens were beautiful. The airport was not crowded and the streets were not crowded. Cars were shining and fast moving.

There were some new faces to receive us but had smiles pasted on them. Courtesies were exchanged and the journey to some destination was interesting to watch people with different colors. Some were white, some black, some red, some brown, some yellow but no purple colored. They had different clothes unlike east and all of it appealed to me. Our residence had a lobby covered by glass panels and the doorman saluted me, as though I was a princess from some unknown province.

The elevator doesn't seem to stop and kept rising and rising, until at last it halted and we were shoved into another lobby like place with glass panels and holding a scenic landscape. It was our would-be home, which didn't have fans about which I have disclosed earlier. There was sea shore at one side, sky scrapers on one side and dwelling tops on the third side. The house was clean and elegant looking.

The breakfast was already decorated on the table and looked good. But I was not hungry after what was served to us at the plane and didn't have my bowel movement. Otherwise everything was new and bright. I was not introduced to anybody in particular but I was showered enough hugs and attention. That was important to me and would remain so later.

It was a planned visit, no not visit but migration, no not even migration considering my US passport, it was simple plan for my return to my place of birth and a plan was already made out by elders. I was happy with the change and more so, when I was put to private school with white kids and black teachers. There were plenty of toys and PT times for enjoyment. I liked going to school without uniform and with the clothes I liked including sneakers.

The only problem was the slang of the language spoken with added suffering of the slang of black teachers, who almost used to chew words before speaking. I was learning and so, the fact that I just came from the east gave me some privileges but not advantages. As such I didn't want to take the advantage of any situation I am put into and that was a gift from Momma, who was of similar type. No, I was her type and not she being my type. It was like asking which came first, the hen or the egg.

I was having some personal troubles. Good thing Guard was not around, otherwise he wouldn't have agreed to it. In his books kids cannot have personal problems except illnesses which again becomes parent's problem. Kids can only have academic problems and problems of learning. But now that he was not to be involved I wanted to share them with Momma and Dad and selected next weekend. I was disappointed to find Momma busy on phone and Dad watching ice hockey on sports channel. I wanted to avoid Aunt because she will have a ready-made speech about do's and don'ts to listen to for a lengthy time.

Instead I was carried to the Zoo. How different it was from the one I was carried in the east. The animals were of larger size and a bit indifferent towards the watchers. There were not many monkeys doing gymnastics and not many Hippos or Rhinos. But the trip was thoroughly satisfying. More so after the gummies and candies and popsicles, which were given to me to hang on.

I was beginning to like the place and the evening strolls in the parks, with swings and slopes. I also liked the bakery cup cakes and ice-cream cones of varying flavors. I liked the McDonalds and visits to Chinese restaurants and relished the soups and noodles with delicious sauces. The place appeared to be worth living. Our building had a separate swimming pool and the water was warm and cozy. There were plenty of cute dogs and some not very cute too. They had leashes long and short and were seeing the kids playing around with jealousy, maybe because kids were not put to leashes and free to run distances and do somersaulting or other fun activities.

Visits to museums and aquariums were equal fun. The museum statues didn't interest me but the variety of sea animals and fishes of varying colors and designs were good to watch. I was equally pleased by the number of parties thrown at our place. The guests would be strangers to me but I was not a stranger to them. The way they would pat at my back or squeeze my cheeks were expressions of intimacy to me. The attention which I would get was the most gratifying. Who doesn't want attention. People wear designer's clothes for the same reason.

I recollected the incidence described by Guard that once during the fasting month's daytime, one Anglo-Indian found one Sikh community man eating a sandwich in the street and it seemed he commented after mistaking his turban and his beard that he must be a Muslim, 'You should be eating now', and he got a spontaneously prepared reply that he is Sikh and then the Anglo-Indian apologetically told him to get well soon and walked passed him.

The incidence reminded of the east and how Guard used to remain occupied during the season of FIFA world cup football matches, which used to be telecasted in this time of year once every 4-5 years. He was fond of watching football, which was a game not as popular as cricket there. Cricket was played on streets, cross roads, backyards, front yards, indoors and outdoors and in any open space enough to through the ball and be able to bat.

Here people seem to be crazy about basketball, baseball, American football where players would wear armored dresses and dash with one another. Difference of culture was marked and I found it remarkably different. In summers every one belonging to all ages and all genders would be wearing shorts. Old fat ladies with shorts could have been ridiculed in the west. Guard always used to say respect the laws of the land. What exactly he meant was difficult for me to interpret, but who would not respect the laws of any land.

Moreover, as shown here on TV, the movies with gun violence and other western thrillers where guns pop up out of the blue and flashes of light thrown from the barrels. I was into violent movies and breaking the laws. I knew the constitution is made of laws, which have to be respected. I was not a 'coy-boy' girl to ride on horses in the dust ridden lanes of the old-time villages.

One fine morning suddenly my older sister came from London and her visit followed a lot of activity. She appeared thin, lean and slim teenager but a nice person by heart. She expressed a lot of emotion towards me and Momma. Dad became even more very busy in moving around and carrying us to downtown, amusement parks and a bigger zoological park with more animals than trees. I liked the bridge which opens up in the middle of the stream in the downtown area to allow taller ships to pass by and come back to get joined for the pedestrians and cars to move about.

In the bigger Zoo I recollected the story told by Guard that once there was a marriage party of the tiger in the jungle and all animals were invited for the celebration. They sang and had a get together with laughter and cries. On the stage one mouse was dancing in the most haphazardly fashion and one goat could not stop him from restraining that mouse by telling him that it is tiger's marriage and he need not get excited so wildly. The mouse didn't stop dancing and made a face and uttered loudly that before his marriage he was a tiger too.

Then Guard had stopped and I asked him to explain and he raised his shoulders to express resignation. I was angry at Guard for telling me non-understandable stories. He later explained to me that it was symbolic and it meant before marriage tiger can dictate terms but after marriage his wife will dictate him making him as good as a mouse and I laughed like I would choke and enjoyed the joke fully well.

He added 'Mom, that doesn't mean you should do the same'. I failed to understand whether he was referring to dictating terms or dancing awkwardly. I felt like dancing then.

Time went by so quickly while my elder sister was around. She was a sweet company and spicy companion during her short visit to our place. Everyone was in happy mood more so me and I will not hesitate to tell that it was me, I was more concerned about. Unlike Grandma who would be concerned about everyone else except herself. She was a nice lady and thorough gentle person, the qualities which Momma inherited from her. Wasn't I being lucky girl? She had an abnormal attachment towards me, duly present when I was born and duly present when I needed her most and parted with me as a person would part with one's life time savings.

Guard used a different word for abnormal. He used to say she had a pathological attachment towards me. I think most of the grand parents love grand children more than their own, because they grow wiser with age and realizes what they have missed out with their children. People say it is likeness, to interest more than the principal, which of course I do not understand.

Guard was different. He had normal attachment towards me and he would use the word physiological. He likes to use hard words always. A cranky old dictionary who reserves hard words in itself. But he had strong feelings for old time culture and its good values. He said once his friend GC borrowed a scooter from his friend and must be speeding while being excited to drive with his wife on the back seat and accidentally hit an old lady from some village.

He was perplexed more than guilty for his faulty driving and failing to apply brakes when he needed most as he was probably looking back at his wife with pride for giving her a scooter ride. He halted and about to pull his scooter on the central stand that the old lady asked for forgiveness when she said 'It is not your mistake as I could not see properly while crossing the street'. So, that was the culture he appreciated. I think his friend GC, Grand Canyon, a better name for him should have been penalized.

Guard would use hard words, better still difficult words even while he would speak his mother tongue or local dialect. He himself translated once to me that once he wanted to tell the cable operator of his colony's TV channels that he was tired of seeing the tired face of the genuinely tired cable operated, upon which that man misunderstood it as a vulgar word and complained to Grandma about, who then interpreted what actually Guard intended and the man was put at ease.

Such was the melodramatic person Guard used to be. I got drifted in my thoughts. I was talking about my elder sister who came and went like an early morning breeze which refreshes someone for a brief time only. I missed her a lot and sent her some seasons greeting cards later. I was back to school routine and weekend outings. I liked to go walking to the school with Momma behind me video shooting my gait or joy of early morning walks.

On some weekend we went to some place with a fancy name somewhere in down town to a spot from where one could see the entire city. I stood there enjoying the view and almost refused to ride back home, but it was not refusing milk and getting away with. Some time later my black teacher with whom I was getting familiar with in person and in slang, recommended another eye test for my glasses. I was carried to friend of Dad who was an expert in fixing the sight with some new advanced medical gadgets and I was given a new number for my glasses.

I got a new one with shell frame and I could see thing more clearly, better than others. I saw the spots and pimple scar on my Aunt's face and informed her, without noting that it had embarrassed her but she kept her cool. She also liked this new-found land interesting and was in good moods, that is why she ignored my uncalled-for comments based on my improved eye-sight. Actually, I had crossed my limits with regards to hurting other's feelings.

Soon the FIFA world cup football season came. But here it was not called football and instead called 'Soccer', as though it is not played with feet. These people are peculiar for renaming things. They would name period for full stops and parenthesis for brackets and instead of asking us to byheart tables like 'two two za four' they would say 'two times two four'. Let them do whatever they wish. They have the liberty to do what they want.

After placing the famous 'Liberty Statue' some where in the east coast they can feel liberated. I don't mind their taking too many liberties with too many things. I don't want them to take liberties with me, that's all. I don't want people to seek answers to their questions from me. Rather they should answer to my questions. Momma sometimes used to get fed up with my questions, which Dad never did.

I always wanted to seek answers for the lack of clarity of my dreams, sometimes pleasing and some times not. People hold me from going into lakeshore more so into the waves to cool off, even if I get wet and expect me to behave like a normal child deprived of her rights. These are funny people whom I feel sympathy at times, as they can sow thorns and expect roses to bud up from them. We are kids of modern times and we will not be kidded by pranks or whole lies or half-truths.

We want proper answers to our improper questions. People are crazy and not us, as we don't want hide behind the veil of tricks and gimmicks. I sometimes feel I should leave them alone and build a world of my own to live my way. They give faulty promises to while away their time and the fragrance of our rewards are lost in this manner. It was as though we are living in stone ages and are being refrained from throwing stones at the houses made of glass.

I was like a little bird who was flying high swaying with the wind and after reaching some height and upon looking down find the world a tiny place cramped with ants. They are not love mongers, they are hate mongers and that is why the hate crimes were increasing in this place, as Dad told me once. I will not allow this to happen and I will become a wall to prevent such happenings. People want to climb over one another to get things which they want but I will not allow them to do so. I will break their speed and pull them down, if I can afford.

I am now beginning to understand people, but I don't want to get late in doing so, that my color gets faded during this time. I some time feel when I want to fly high like that bird these people may not hesitate to cut my feathers to disallow my steep rise. I was not like those who would rest in the middle before reaching destinations, I am of the type who could continue moving until I reach my destination, as so often I hear from GPS voice directions in Momma's car, until I hear that we have reached our destination.

When I look at the lake shore from one of the glass panels of our home and see no tides coming towards me I lose interest in them, I want tides to go higher and higher until they reach me, even if I am at home just looking out. I was not informed correctly about this place when I was told that here people don't tell lies, they don't act mean and that what efforts one takes here are rewarded. It was not the case with me or there was something wrong with me or people around me.

I get switched off like a bulb which got fused when someone tell lies to me. I was asked to take deep breaths whenever I get angry, but deep breaths are not like ointments which relieve pain. I wanted to be clear in my spellings, grammar and comprehension of English and I wanted the math tables to slowly creep into my brain on their own and remain there forever. If someone tries to pull my legs I will rise above them and do the same.

So, I was talking about the world soccer tournament, which was shown on our TV at odd times. The same was the case in the east, when Guard was seen watching games when I go to sleep and was seen watching when I used to get up. Doesn't he sleep was my question put to him bluntly. He felt cornered and escaped by telling me yet another story about his friend GC. It seems GC was watching games with his neighbor on his TV at his place, not GC's and he ignored his wife sending messenger to return back.

After several summons, his wife got steamed up and gave GC last warning through the messenger boys. Upon finding GC's fault obviously, she went to the neighbor's house and showed GC a red card. Guard became silent and I wanted the story to be completed. Then it seems GC had to leave the room like a player had to leave the field upon being shown a red card. I knew his wife was a smart lady who knew how to handle her stubborn husband.

Time had wings and it flew in no time. In no time my grand parents visited us from the east and they were placed in my room. Well, my room as such was a mess and got messed up even more. Good thing I was accustomed to share living with them and was aware of their habits. Maybe for a day or two I had difficulty then it became a routine. After sometime I started liking the arrangement. I was on the top of the bunk bed, Guard at the bottom and Grandma preferred sleeping on the carpeted floor.

The timings were perfect and the routine was jubilant. Aunt had to adjust in the ante-room, which was small but held privacy for her. Me and Guard used to go in the mornings for a stroll in the park across the road and Grandma used to join us at times. When she would come down we would hold 50-100 yards race and I used to win every time. There were other people with their pet dogs around but kept some distance.

After breakfast we would get ready to go to city center where Momma had her boutique, spend some time, play around, go for window shopping sprees and return to find some guests to interact and exchange pleasantries and would order lunch from nearby restaurants and go home in the evening. We also attended some parties thrown elsewhere and visited places of interest for all like malls, theatres, long drives and amusement parks.

It was all fun and joy for me. Weather as usual was unpredictable but not harsh. There were plenty of familiar faces around and many shops belonging to our community. Time was well spent and lot of photos were added to my album. I also got a girl's bike to ride in the backyard and parking lot and in hot afternoons we used to throw stream of hose pipe's water on one another and make a festival out of it. We watched air shows and parades. I could also wear dresses brought from east and showed off to people around.

The elders were also searching alliances for the Aunt, who was already a graduate in biotechnology. A lot of locals jumped at the chances and the number of guests increased many folds. Aunt was a smart lady and naturally expected a suitable match. Young men with different backgrounds and different careers attended us and were rejected by one or the other of the elders.

My paternal grandparents were of big help in the search but nothing materialized. I was also casually asked to give my opinion and I could favor any one of them. I thought all of them put together also could not equal the beauty, qualification, poise and presence of her. Some serious discussions were going on and some serious decisions were taking place. We were not in any hurry as she was still young and looked even younger.

Then it so happened that she got an offer of admission into a celebrity university affiliated college for post-graduation and then alliance search was postponed for the time being. Guard and Aunt left early to meet up with her admission requirements and Grandma was left back to continue giving us company. She prepared some very delicious cuisines for all of us and we liked the food and the company. We watched TV and movies and I started going to school after the vacations.

Momma got busy with the routine of dropping and picking me for school, help me in home work, along side managing the store. Dad used to leave very early for work and would return in the afternoons for lunch and only then we moved out for other activities. After sometime Grandma also left and the house appeared vacant for few days. But the show has to go on and life has to be lived with the allocated responsibilities and tasks.

There was judicious distribution of rest, relaxation, recreation but with priority to my studies and school progress. I was picking up but not up to the standardized criteria of grades. There were no ranks allocated at school except grades of ABC. I was having difficulty with math and a private online tutor was hired to give tuitions on skype. The lady was from Canada and helped in wasting my and her time and I kept getting B grade in math. Dad had no time and Momma had no time for my homework assignments.

Dad had changed his parent organization standard his own company, hence got extra busy. He would have to do field work and desk work all by himself and could listen to grievances without even registering them properly. I couldn't blame him. I couldn't blame Momma also for poor lady she has plenty of pending work to complete and also was obliged to increase the profit margins, I think.

It was too much and I was contended with self help and even hated the public school where I was shifted for its good reputation. The state syllabus was a task and the weight of the back pack kept increasing, with not much going to my head. I started compensating by trying to please teachers and others and managed to pull on. I heard the news about Momma's baby bump and she was asked to take precautions.

I couldn't notice any change until a later time when her walk was waddling like a duck and her baby bump kept increasing in dimensions. I was curious about the new arrival. Whether I would be getting a baby sister or brother. I preferred a sister, as I was unhappy with the notoriety of boys I encountered. My grand parents also returned well in time to help Momma, but this not as visitors but as immigrants and it was big change.

They were placed in the city center in a separate apartment with all found and I was blessed by two homes to bank upon. Better still is I had two shelters, as though I am a homeless with options to chose among both. On weekdays I would be at the shore and on weekends I will remain in the city center. That is how my conditions changed towards better or worse, it was not easy to settle with.

'What goes around comes around', what a phrase which Momma uses time and again. What exactly she means by that I am afraid to ask. She was doing hard work and making a lot of progress in her business. she was practically expanding as Dad did in his profession. This is a capitalistic country, with capitalistic dreams, capitalistic economics, capitalistic chaos. I was not sure how it would shape up when I grow up to be an adult, to become a part of this capitalistic society. What will come around will be faced around accordingly. As for the present I was happy with this family reunion and soon my Uncle from NZ to join with my cute cousin sister, who was like her mother and always laughing.

I was only getting worried about Guard. He was not active anymore, not humorous anymore and not fit for work or travel. He would remain domiciled in his room either thinking or writing his books. What is the target he has kept about the number of books he planned for his short future? I am sure he will not survive for long, more so with the ailments adding to his list of prevailing conditions. Good thing he has not got into dementia and still encourages me and now, my younger sister included. But I still don't like his teaching discipline to both of us. We are children and he should keep his teachings of discipline to the elders.

I remembered his old-time friend a bald headed obese but hilarious character, who would not miss a day in making visits to Guard. There was 100% attendance to his credit immaterial of his health, weather or timings. He was in habit of calling Guard by name from the gate before entering. One day I was angry and shouted from inside that Guard is not at home, but still he came in and giggled like a teenager boy and caught me and tickled me to laughter. He was a nice man and a good man, either doesn't understand or doesn't mind being ridiculed. May God rest his soul in peace.

One day Guard suffered a stroke on the same weaker side and somehow managed to walk down, leaned across the lamp post, hailed a cab and went to ER where he was put to trolley as though he was brought after calling 911 and put to hospital for investigations, diagnosed and was being treated when left against medical advice and came home because of his habit of smoking pipe which of course was prohibited there. Since then he started swallowing a hand full of tablets and continued with smoking. What a joker he had proved himself.

Grandma changed our pet cat because of some reason and brought a new one, who became friendly with me soon enough. She was not as playful as the previous one, but it didn't bother me because at least I had a replacement instead of nothing and I was happy for both of us. I was also happy because my unit shifted to a new premises and life became even more busy, we visiting 3 homes almost every day. Good thing my summer vacations started and one visit to school was spared. Grandma occupied another room but used to peep into Guard's room as often as she could and to be reminding me of stray cats peeping into domestic cats as often.

Grandma still was cooking her delicacies and satisfying our hunger and satiety too. She stopped sweets and junk food and I cursed her for this unwelcomed change. She was gaining weight but that didn't make any difference to her as she continued changing her dresses every day. If she could help she may change or shed her skin every day. What a stimulating person she was. The point of further interest was she would ask us to change our dresses every day. I wish she could fill my small wardrobe with 365 dresses to last me a year. But there are certain things which cannot be helped, was an oft repeated phrase for me.

I only felt sorry for Guard for his inability to continue with his eastern routine for lack of licensure. This sympathy led me to recollect all those hear-say stories of his past adventures he displayed in the career building. I believe one lady patient was in ICU for few days and doctors of that hospital were unable to reason out her apparent unconsciousness.

One of Guard's disciples notified to the hospital administration that they wanted to bring their own specialist for her review. Guard was called and he shifted the patient from ICU to private room and whispered some commands and the patient stood up and was brought down and discharged. I was told later that she was actually suffering from Hysterical coma. I don't know what that means.

There was yet another incident of another lady brought physically restraint because her agitated condition based on some witchcraft done to her. The quack even told the parents of that patient that whom so ever takes the spirit out of her would have to die. Guard did some treatment and she got better. The family was happy but worried that Guard may have to die and kept coming back to enquire about his welfare.

I was at loss to understand the intricacies of Guard's treatment skills. And I don't know

now he was writing books to earn or to pass his time. He couldn't sit idle, I knew for sure. If he is not writing then he is listening to old melodies or singing on his own under his breath. He even tried few sessions of vocal music training for me and my younger sister, which went in vain.

I thought of cheering him up one day and taught my younger sister some gymnastic tricks and we exhibited a show of our so-called circus, which was liked by all and Guard also passed comments like 'Good show' and 'nice circus', etc. but I knew he was not very impressed. He must have had high expectancy levels, I need to repeat his own words. But another day Momma texted a pregnancy report to Dad and he was aghast with bewilderment.

Later he was informed that the report belonged to my Aunt and not Momma and this news definitely cheered Guard's mood and he seemed contented and expressed his gratefulness to God along with praise to the almighty. I was also happy but for a change I wished the new arrival should be a boy instead of a girl, as I was vexed with girls in the family already.

As far as Guard was concerned, I think he was a bit disheartened. Some bit by the worldly favors and the rest by his adverse circumstances. He was expecting that American dream would bring him some relief but when it came to testing it him pain instead. I had a feeling that his heart was aching but he would let it come to his eyes to shed any tears. That was the tradition in which he lived didn't allow him the ways and means of expressing emotions.

He knew he has a family here but he was of the type who wouldn't even depend on his own family. He would prefer hired help which of course he couldn't afford here. I think he used to varied thoughts but somehow, he managed to convince him to live and let others live along side. He must have been getting questions or rather asking him questions himself, without getting any answers. Up till in the recent past he was a strong pillar of support to the society but unfortunately now he was resembling ruins of old times. He proved a fool in the end.

I forget to mention two incidences which better be not recorded because they were actually embarrassing for me. On my birthday, I couldn't remember which one I was under the effect of sugar rush and was excited, better still restless and I was practically dancing like the mouse in the tiger's wedding and jumped up on the sofa and the on the hand rest and slipped to land on my Uncles lap and looked into his eyes, which were filled with fear and fright.

Good thing he didn't get startled enough to jump on his own to fall back on the sofa. Then I was called to bring my own birthday cake, which gladly did. Only later to realize that it slipped from its base and fell face down and I didn't know how to react, while the elders were occupied in other affairs. I coolly lifted it placed it back and inserted candles haphazardly to hide its rugged cream face.

Life is full of compromises and I was prepared for any eventuality of any circumstance to cope up with. I had become a master in coping up, as I had been coping with all possible challenges which a 7th grader could have been subjected to. Now I was waiting for my 12th B' day soon to come as I was going in teens and promised an iPhone as a gift from Momma.

But of course, conditional to behaving like a good girl as though I had not been so until now. The conditions which sometime elders put on children should be protested like protests I had read in history lessons for civil rights and racial discriminations in the past. I ignored them for the time being, because I didn't want to take any risks at the last moment.

My birthday came on the schedule date, but I was little apprehensive to step up the ladder of teens. I was supposed to behave like one. I was expected to be responsible person of my adolescence and was even carried to the boutique and introduced to designer outfits, one to choose for my big day. I shook off my clouded mood. I also shook off the thought that there would be any pretense in this change. It was to come imminently. But what was to be recognized was the fact that I could no longer be a child.

It should be taken as a refreshing change and should not be held back. I ignored my thoughts and my feelings prepared myself for it. I could get some emotional benefits, who knows. I started learning the business of Momma's boutique. I was asked to differentiate between bought and consigned clothes. I learnt to identify the catalogues and the tags, and to get acquainted with designer's names.

I was shown how to steam the garments on mannequins and hold to fold them in a methodical manner. I learnt the measurements and endorsements of receipts. I practiced how to chart out the sales and orders of pending sales. I was given the additional liability to keep an eye on the sales girls and their activities and to report any deviations. It all seemed a tough job initially but one gets used to things.

I began to understand the routine. How shipments arrive, how they are unpacked and listed and included in the stocks and the inventory Recorded. I also started to include them in the excel sheet and mark their prices, both cost and sales prices. I was beginning to enjoy the given tasks and in the pretext of becoming useful was very satisfying.

I was not allowed to wear ripped tights and even practiced fake smiles for the customers. We had registered clients and casual entries of customers. I was also getting familiar with the potential buyers and virtual window shoppers. It was all new but challenging experience.

I was also obliged to resist showing my emotions on the visitors. Some were celebrities some were ordinary people from the commons. I grinned cheekily to myself, but it was not overwhelming. It was not easy but not difficult as well. The number of visitors increased in summers and I had to exercise the multi-tasking to my capacity. I began to understand the sales through credit or debit cards and how in state and out of states should be taxed accordingly.

I was kept busy for a limited number of hours every day and was also exposed to few clients, who passed on compliments for my appearance and appeal. One customer even casually mentioned that I could as well be a good model, if I learn how to cat walk ramps.

Another customer asked me what I would be doing, if not involved in this training course at any given time and didn't wait for my answer. Some questions are asked casually to be ignored casually. The part of training which I found difficult was the sketches I was supposed to draw for the likes and dislikes of known clients. Up till now I was only drawing the outlines, but now I had to fill in the lines to demarcate cuts and frills and embroidery and embellishments.

One has to earn the benefits to reap the profits after putting a lot of efforts. I was getting ready to put in efforts, not bothering to see the results. Efforts are important than results. Proper efforts will get proper results to become proper rewards. I was asked to venture my first sales and shoved into a crowd of all age ladies. Elegant looking and posed with presence.

I approached them and enquired about the person who needs some guidance for the racks of outfits according to their choice and purpose. I was taken by surprise that the family came looking for a bridal outfit for the sixty plus lady who was ultimately getting married. I showed her the costumes and she selected one after trying in fitting room and required some minor alteration to suit her age. Designers don't make bridals for sixty plus would be brides. I remained courteous in spite of feeling a bit uncomfortable.

The first sales of my teenage life were documented and I felt a sense of pride in me, which again I shook off without getting concerned, but felt happy. I only hoped she will ask for cash back later. My birthday was celebrated. I wore the selected dress and was admired. I cut the cake without spilling it and blew the candles to taste the chunk thrusted into my mouth. It melted in my mouth and the song replayed in the background with patented music meant for 'Happy birthday to you' rhyme.

I was given envelopes with gift checks, gift cards and cash instead for toys or dresses. It suited my taste and the liberty to use the envelopes as I wish. I felt elated and refrained my urgency to open the iPhone box already activated to make my first personal call to Guard who retired early back into his room. I tried again but it rang with no response. I tried for the last time and was redirected to answering tone. I was not getting any apprehensive thoughts, but I kept things to myself. I knew his type, if we wants to avoid he could.

Curiously the FIFA world cup came early this time or may be on the scheduled time, which I found it as earlier. Under the influence of the soccer fever game or under the direction of Guard or all by herself Momma registered me to soccer camp and on the very first day I was declared player of the day, because of my juggling with the ball and headers pointing to the players of my team and my lack of doing any foul plays and strike at the goal with an in-swinging shot at the target, which went into the upper right corner of the net, Goooooaaal.

THEY WERE ALL MAJORING IN PEACE AND CONFLICT STUDIES, SO IT WAS EASY TO LIE AND SAY THAT
A SPECIAL CHEMICAL WE USED IN THE MOLECULAR FOUNDRY LAB. I KNEW NOW THAT WHAT I'D DO
GO AGAIN—AND THAT I COULD EVEN CONTROL IT, AT LEAST A LITTLE. WHILE WE WERE IN THE BACK
WITH EVAPORATING THINGS, TRYING TO MELT TH PLASTIC CUFF PINCHING MY WRISTS. I CONCENT
ENDS HOLDING THEM TOGETHER, TRYING TO RE RODUCE THE FEELING I'D HAD JUST BEFORE THE
MY ARMS WERE FREE, THOUGH BRIEFLY WET. AT THE STATION, ALL OF US WERE PROCESSED AND REL
HAD SOME KIND OF TRUST FUND THAT INVOLVED LAWYERS AND LOTS OF MONEY TO SPEND ON BAI
WHENEVER THEY GOT INTO TROUBLE HE GRE LIBERATION ARMY WASTED NO TIME TURNING ME
THE ECO-AVENGER ORDINARY PEOPLE WHO D ED IN COSTUMES TO FIGHT CRIME WERE ALL THE
OF THE TV SERIES WHO WANTS TO BE A SUPER O? BUT MOST OF THE CITIZEN SUPERHERO VIDEOS
GUYS IN MASKS AND MOTORCYCLE JACKETS YELLING AT POT DEALERS IN SUBURBAN PARKS. MARIA
AND A SKI MASK, AND FILMED WHILE EVAPORATED A E ADDED LITTLE COMIC BOOK BUBBLE
THINGS LIKE "TAKE THAT, ENVIRONMENT-DESTROYING GAS GUZZLER!" OR "ONCE AGAIN, ECO-AVEN
THE CAR MENACE! SHE POSTED ON CITIZEN TES AND GOT HER FRIENDS AT THE E
BLOG TO DO A STORY ABOUT OUR W TUALLY ING LINKED TO ONE OF THE VIDEOS
CITIZEN SUPERHERO ON THE WEB," BECAUSE THE SPECIAL EFFECTS ARE SO GOOD THAT IT REALLY LO
HAS A SUPERPOWER "EVERY TIME I RAN MY HANDS OVER A GUY AND FELT ITS ELECTRONS UNZIP.
WAS ALL THIS DISAPPEARED MASS GOING YOU'D EXPECT THE DEMOLISHED MOLECULAR BONDS TO
TO THROW ME ACROSS THE ROOM, O BUT INSTEAD THERE WAS ONLY A COOL MIST. MAY
NOT DEMOLITION. I COMBED THE WE STORIES OF CARS THAT HAD MATERIALIZED OUT OF NOV
MY WORKING THEORY WAS THAT MY POWERS OF DESTRUCTION ED TO AFFECT BOTH MASS AN
WEIRD KIND OF SENSE, BUT IT DIDN'T GET ANY CLOSER TO FIGU OUT WHAT HAD HAPPENED T
DEGREE AND TOOK A RESEARCH JOB MOLECULAR FOUN CHURNING OUT INVISIBLE SHEE
THE PRINCIPAL INVESTIGATOR IN CHARGE OF THE LAB MARVELED AT MY DEDICATION TO THE JOB. M
POLYMERS ACROSS A GOLD SUBSTRATE, BUT IT WAS ALL SELF-SERVING. I WAS TRYING TO REVERSE
AT THE LAB ALLOWED ME TO TARGET OBJECTS WITH AN EXTREME DEGREE OF GRANULARITY. I CO
GREEN LIBERATION ARMY, BUT THOSE EXPERIMENTS WEREN'T PARTICULARLY HELPFUL WHEN I CA
FINGERS. I NEVER KNEW EXACTLY WHAT I WAS DOING. WHO KNEW WHAT SUBSTANCES WERE IN T
ISOLATE AND DISINTEGRATE, AND JUST MAYBE REGENERATE. AT LAST, EARLY ONE I BEGAN
ROLL MY OWN CARBON NANOTUBE. I GOT SO EXCITED THAT I WAS OUT OF EXISTENC
PAINSTAKINGLY, OVER A PERIOD OF MONTHS, I BEGAN TO WORK ON MORE COMPLICATED OBJECTS
AIR AND LUNG TISSUE OUT OF SALT. WHEN I FELT A SOLID OBJECT CURLING OUT OF THE ATOMS IN
SUBSTANCE COMING FROM EVERYTHING I HAD TAKEN APART AND SENT WHIRLING INTO SUBATOMIC
HAD DISAPPEARED WAS COMING BACK TO ME. IN SPRING, I RETURNED TO THE TOWN WHERE LAWR
AGO, ALMOST TO THE WEEK. I HAD REDUCED LAWRENCE TO VAPOR. NOW I WOULD USE MY POWER
SUBATOMIC PARTICLES HE'D LEFT BETWEEN THOSE TWO TRASH BINS. THE CONCRETE HAD BEEN
AGO, AND THE DONUT SHOP WAS GONE. IT DIDN'T MATTER. I STOOD IN THE MIDDLE OF THE PARKI
THAT MOVED THROUGH ME. CLOSING MY EYES, I EXTENDED MY ARMS AND I REMEMBERED HOW IT FE
LAWRENCE'S BODY. HIS HAIR WAS THICK. HIS COLLAR BONE SHARP, VEINS RAN IN SOFT BULGES DO
HIS MUSCLES WERE ALWAYS BUNCHED INTO HYPERVIGILANCE. I TASTED HIM MY MOUTH. I TRANS
AT FIRST I WAS UNCERTAIN, BUT THEN I COULD FEEL THE SHREDS OF HIS MOLECULAR STRUCTURE A
OUT OF NOTHING INTO MY WAITING HANDS. THE AIR GREW CLOUDY WITH HIS ASSEMBLING TISSUE
WAS EMERGING INTO NAKED, WET SOLIDITY, JUST AS I COULD SEE THE OUTLINE OF HIS FACE, HIS
A COOLING SOLID WHICH I COULD BARELY CONTROL. THERE WAS ONLY ONE THING I COULD DO. FI
I HAD CONJURED FROM DISPERSING. EXTEMPORIZE. I GATHERED WHAT REMAINED OF HIM BETWEEN
HANDS, SQUEEZING HIS PARTICLES A DENSE TORUS. WHAT I CHANGED TO THE GROUND
GOLD WEDDING BAND. LAWRENCE COULD FIT ON MY RING FINGER, BUT HE W ED AS MUCH AS
THING, DRAGGING HIM HOME. I OUGHT LAWRENCE TO WORK INSIDE A REINFORCED STEEL BOX T
I HAD A LOT OF CRAZY IDEAS, THOUGHTS ABOUT HOW I COULD REBUILD HIM. MAYBE I COULD
OUT OF THE MINERAL-RICH EARTH? OR BRING TO ENGINEERING LAB, AND TR
EXISTING FLESH I WAS CONTENT LATTICE THESE POSSIBILITIES WHEN MARIA SENT ME A TEXT. S
ON A FEATURE, TONIGHT WOULD BE OUR LAST CAR DISINTEGRATION VIDEO. "CAN U MEET
OUT?" SHE ASKED. I COULD. WHEN I ARRIVED, PULLING LAWRENCE BEHIND ME, SHE WAS THE ONLY
MEMBERS OF THE GREEN LIBERATION ARMY WERE APPARENTLY AT THEIR OFFICE JOBS. MA
BRAND-NEW RAV4, EATING SALAD OUT OF A PLASTIC YOGURT CONTAINER. "DO YOU THINK YO
WHILE IT'S MOVING?" SHE WOULD BE SO COOL TO SHOW THE CAR ROTTING FROM
THE CAMERA ON THE DASHBOARD AND DRIVING AS RIA EXPLA
BLOCKED OUT EACH SHOT SOMEBODY
MARIA DIDN'T KNOW THAT MY POWER CAME FROM BEYOND THE UNDERSTANDING OF
USE IT MORE THAN ANYONE, AND UNTIL TODAY, SHE'D ALWAYS WANTED MORE ORE I
MY HANDS ON HER BARE ARMS AND KISSED HER ON THE MOUTH. "THIS IS OUR LAST VIDEO, LET
I SAID SHE DIDN'T LOOK SURPRISED. WE OPENED THE HATCHBACK AND PULLED OURSELVES INSIDE
IN BEHIND US, THE HANDCART BANGING OVER THE BUMPER. SOMEHOW I WORKED IT OUT OF
SPACE. AS I KISSED HER NECK, I THOUGHT ABOUT HOW ALL HUMAN SKIN FEELS MORE OR LESS THE

rinted in the United States
y Bookmasters